Vacationland

Margit Ausbruch-Newman

Vacationland

A HALF CENTURY SUMMERING IN MAINE

David E. Morine

DOWN EAST BOOKS

Slightly different versions of the following stories have appeared in various publications:

In *Down East* magazine: "Dad's Humongous Pickerel" (originally titled "Always Grab the Leader"), "Just Lookin' for Fish," "The Rudy Vallee Defense," "One Over Our Limit," "Breaking Even," "My Last Hurrah," "Home Free," "Always Leave the Keys with the Car," "Moose Mainea," "Make Way for Jet Skis"

In *Sports Illustrated:* "Absolute Loonacy"

In *Reader's Digest:* "Home Free"

In *Amherst* magazine: "Golfing with the Bishop"

In *Good Dirt: Confessions of a Conservationist,* by David E. Morine (Globe Pequot Press, 1990; Ballantine Books, 1993): "Just Lookin' for Fish," "One Over Our Limit," "Absolute Loonacy," "Dad's Humongous Pickerel" ("Always Grab the Leader")

ISBN 0-89272-538-9
Library of Congress Catalog Card Number 2001091610
Cover illustration by Scott Earle
Printed at Versa Press

2   4   5   3   1

DOWN EAST BOOKS
P.O. BOX 679, CAMDEN, MAINE 04843

Book orders: 1-800-766-1670
e-mail: books@downeast.com

To Ted and Bill and Ruth,
thanks for not challenging my memory.

CONTENTS

ACKNOWLEDGMENTS

My sincere appreciation and admiration to Mary and Sue Jordan and their mother, Ellen, for guiding me through my early years in Vacationland; Pam Lord Bliss, the warden's daughter, for keeping me honest in Lovell; Howard Corwin for letting me know what the Greater Lovell Land Trust is doing; Charlie Taylor for making sure that my words are processed and legal; Dave Thomas and Dale Kuhnert for bringing a little of western Maine Down East; Ruth Morine and Susan Flint for their proofing and flattery; Neale Sweet, Karin Womer, and Terry Brégy at Down East Books for permitting me to talk about their state; and, finally, Paul Flint for doing what he always does. I just write this stuff. It's Paul who makes it readable. If you find anything in *Vacationland* that you enjoy, Paul undoubtedly had a hand in it.

CROSSING THE LINE

My love affair with Maine started in the summer of '46. I was three. Dad had just gotten back from winning the war, and we were living with my mother's parents, William and Florence Tee, in their big house on Pleasant Street in Arlington, Massachusetts. My mother's whole family was living there, except for Uncle Kirby. He was living with his in-laws around the corner. In addition to my mother; my father; my older brother, Ted; and me, there were Aunt Mary and Aunt Florence; Uncle Arthur; two cousins, Carol and Richard; and Great Gramma Kirby. Dad was looking for a place of our own, but thanks to the war, there was nothing available, at least not at our price. Not that it mattered to me. I liked living at Grampa and Gramma's. There was always something happening. I was never by myself, people were coming and going, and somebody was always having a birthday. But there was no privacy. With the war over, Mom and Dad wanted their own house. They wanted to get on with their lives.

For Dad's vacation, Mom decided that we should get away. Grampa always had a long list of chores he wanted done, and she must have realized that cutting the lawn, weeding the garden, trimming the hedges, washing the car, painting the steps, and cleaning the cellar wouldn't be much of a vacation for Dad. Mom had found an ad in the *Boston Herald* for some camps in Fryeburg, Maine. The ad said to write Rev. Jack Jordan. Mom was a good Episcopalian and figured the camps must be nice if they were run by a reverend. Dad hated the thought of dipping into our savings, but the price was right, fifteen dollars a week, so he agreed.

We had such a good time at Jordan's that we kept going back every summer. Dad always reserved the same cabin, Little Beaver, for the first two weeks in July. He liked going to Maine early in July. The days were long, which gave us more time for fishing, and because we were the first campers of the season, Reverend Jordan let us arrive on Friday night, the day before the camps officially opened.

On the last Friday in June, Mom, Ted, and I would get up at first light to start packing. Dad would get home an hour or two early from his job at the Department of Education, at 200 Newbury Street in Boston. We'd load up the car and head north, up Route 28 to Andover, then catch 125 through Haverhill into New Hampshire. When we came to Rochester, we'd stop at Colby's Family Restaurant. I was a little husky, and that was a big treat for me. I'd have the turkey dinner with mashed potatoes and lots of hot buttered rolls. For dessert, Dad would order us each a piece of Colby's famous banana cream pie. Then he'd buy another whole pie to go.

"Don't you boys sit on this box," he'd say, carefully packing the pie into the already overloaded car. For Dad, a Colby's banana cream pie was a vacation unto itself.

By now, it would be getting dark, so I'd crawl onto the ledge under the back window and doze. I'd be too excited to sleep and too tired to stay awake. I could tell when we were going through the Ossipees. Over the hum of the tires, I'd hear Mom saying, "Jack, slow down, you'll get a ticket." Dad would laugh and say, "Relax, Donna, there's not a cop within twenty miles of here. This is no-man's-land."

I'd sit up when we got to Conway around eleven o'clock. Conway was the last town in New Hampshire, and Fryeburg was just over the line. "There's Maine!" Dad would say, flashing his high beams at the sign. Ted and I would lean out the windows, the wind blowing in our faces, reaching forward as far as we could, trying to be the first in Maine.

> ### Welcome to Maine
> ### Vacationland

"I win, I win!" I'd yell as we zipped past the sign. I always had to be the first in Maine. It had been six hours since we'd left home, but we'd crossed the line; we'd entered the wilds of Maine. The first thing Dad would do was slow down so we could read the fire alert, a big cutout of Smokey the Bear. A bubble over Smokey's hat read, "Remember, only you can prevent forest fires," and there was an arrow next to his shovel that pointed to the fire danger level—high, medium, or low. The image of a wildfire, like the one in *Bambi*, would rage through my head, and that was pretty scary.

"Looks like they rolled up the sidewalks," Dad would say as we eased into Fryeburg. All the stores were closed and most of the houses dark. The lights that were still on silhouetted the massive elms that lined both sides of the street. "Everything looks the same," Mom would say as we passed Solari's General Store, Oliver's Rexall Drugs, and the Blacksmith Shop, which was now a restaurant. "There's the house of the guy who writes

Hopalong Cassidy," Ted would say. Although the writer of *Hopalong Cassidy* was Fryeburg's greatest celebrity, nobody ever seemed to know his name.

At the monument in the middle of town, the one honoring John Stevens, an early settler who spent the winter of 1762–63 in Fryeburg, Dad would turn east on Route 113, the main road to Portland. There was no need to slow down; there were no traffic lights in Fryeburg. "They must have had a good winter," Mom would say as we passed a streetlight. "All the houses look painted." Freshly painted houses were Mom's way of assessing the local economy.

We crept past the bank, the Gulf station, Emerson's Red and White, the Dairy Joy, Trumball's Hardware, Holden Ford, Kenerson's Barber Shop, Hastings Law Office, the registry of deeds, the post office, and the "doughnut tree," a huge elm with its bottom branch twisted around like a doughnut. Dad started picking up speed down the hill past the log pond at Diamond Match. "Smell the wood," he'd say, taking in a deep breath. We'd all take in a deep breath, then let out a contented *"ahhhh"* as we exhaled freshly cut pine.

Now came the best part, the straightaway by the airport. For a main route, 113 wasn't much of a road. It went up and down like a roller coaster, and Dad would gun the engine so we'd fly over the humps. Ted and I would be bouncing up and down in the back seat, screaming, "Faster, Dad. Go faster!" Mom would be yelling, "Jack, slow down! We'll go off the road."

After the airport, Dad did slow down. That's when we started passing the camp roads to Lovewell Pond. "Watch for Jordan's," he'd say.

"There it is!" Ted and I would shout as the headlights lit a tree with a little hand-lettered sign that read "Jordan's Camps."

When Dad turned the car down the little sandy road, it was like Alice falling down the rabbit hole. The high beams cut a tunnel through the deep and dark and silent woods. We'd bump around the twists and turns, all the time leaning forward, looking for the reflection from the eyes of a deer, moose, or even a bear caught in the headlights. At the final bend, the lights would illuminate eight little green cabins nestled under the majestic pines. It looked like Wonderland, and it was.

Dad would pull into an opening right above Little Beaver. Ted and I would tumble out onto a cool carpet of pine needles. We'd all pause for a moment listening to the stillness. For one night, we had the camps all to ourselves.

"All right, boys, let's get moving," Mom would say. "I'll make up the beds while you unload the car. The sheets and blankets are in that Campbell's Soup box." Before we left for Maine, we'd go to the A&P and ask the manager for some used boxes. Mom knew where everything was by the brand names on the boxes.

"Where's my fishing rod?" "Forget about your rod and take this box in to your mother." "Dad, Ted took my bag." "That's my bag, stupid." "Here, you take this banana cream pie, and be very careful." "Mom, which bed is mine?" "You and Ted are in here." "Ted always gets the best side." "That's because I'm older." "Okay, it's late. You boys hop into bed. You've got a big day tomorrow."

The year I was eight, it was unusually hot when we arrived. "Dad, we can't sleep," Ted said after we'd gone to bed. "It's too hot."

"You're too excited," Dad said. "But it *is* hot. What do you say we all go for a swim?"

"Yeah!"

Mom dug into a Wheaties box and pulled out our suits, new ones printed like leopard skins. Ted had gotten the idea for leopard-skin suits from watching Johnny Weismuller in a Tarzan movie. Mom had searched all over Boston before she finally found them in a discount bin at Filene's Basement.

Dad grabbed a gray navy-surplus lantern and led us along the rocky path to the beach. A loon's mournful cry rose from the bog. Across the lake a lone light flickered from Trebor, one of the two girls' camps on Lovewell Pond. In the moonlight we counted eight wooden boats pulled up along the shore, one for each cabin.

"The water feels like silk," Mom said, easing in. We all eased in. Mom was right; it did feel like silk, soft and smooth and inviting. This was the best moment my family ever had—swimming in Lovewell Pond, late at night, on the last Friday in June 1951.

Once we were over the line, Ted and I had chores, but they were nothing like the chores we had at home. At home, we had to take out the garbage, sweep the cellar stairs, mow the lawn. In Maine, we had to get wood for the stove, ice for the refrigerator, water for drinking.

Getting the wood was easy. The woodshed was right in the middle of camp. At the start of each summer, Reverend Jordan would fill the shed with a truckload of scraps from a dowel factory in Brownfield. We'd walk into the shed, Ted would hold out his arms, and I'd stack up the dowels.

Getting the ice was a little harder. We'd go into the icehouse behind the shed where Reverend Jordan stored the boats, scrape the sawdust off a block of ice, and slide it into the wheelbarrow. We were too little to use the tongs, but once we got the block into the barrow, we could wheel it home.

Getting the water, that was tough. The spring was a long quarter mile back in the woods at the base of a hemlock gully. The gully was deep and damp and home to deerflies, horseflies, and hordes of mosquitoes that lived to feast on kids from Jordan's. Reverend Jordan provided used kerosene bottles for the water. Back in the fifties, there was no Environmental Protection Agency, and nobody saw anything strange about putting drinking water in used kerosene jugs. These round, glass gallon jugs had a neck no more than an inch in diameter. This meant that we had to hold the jugs under the surface until all the air was forced out. The water in the spring was freezing, and our hands would go numb long before the jugs were filled.

We'd stop at the top of the gully and Ted would say, "Davey, you fill while I swat." Filling the jugs was a lot harder than swatting the bugs, but I never argued. Everybody knew you had to do what your big brother told you. We'd sprint down the path, and while Ted flipped back the wooden cover to the spring, I'd unscrew the caps to the jugs. Then Ted would start swatting and I'd start filling. The water was so clear that at first I'd think the spring was empty. That misperception would be clarified when a stinging cold shot up my arm. *Glog, glog, glog*—bubbles would start trickling to the surface. I'd feel the mosquitoes in my mouth, my eyes, my nose, my ears, my hair, all buzzing away enjoying their feast.

Whap, whap, whap, whap. Ted would be pounding me on my head, my back, my arms, my legs. "Hurry up, Davey," he'd say. "I'm gettin' eaten alive."

"You?" I'd scream. "What about me?"

Once a jug was half filled, it would stay under the surface by itself. *Glug, glug, glug.* I'd grit my teeth and hold on. One jug, two jugs, three, four. At last, all four would be filled and I'd jump up, my numb hands flailing around my head trying to clear the biting, buzzing cloud. While I fumbled with the caps, Ted closed the cover. Then we'd each grab two jugs and start up the path. With a jug in each hand, we were defenseless. Deerflies and horseflies attacked our heads while swarms of mosquitoes coated our arms and legs. Once out of the gully, we could outrun the mosquitoes, but the deerflies and the horseflies wouldn't give up. They'd keep buzzing around us all the way back to camp.

Every hundred yards or so we'd have to stop to put down the jugs. The only way to carry a kerosene jug was by slipping an index finger through the glass loop at the neck. After a hundred yards, the ends of our fingers felt as though they were being pulled out of our knuckles. It wasn't until we were back on the screen porch sipping a glass of ice-cold spring water that our chores were done.

One of the best things about crossing the line was the change that came over Dad. At home, he was always working and worrying about money, but at Jordan's he was relaxed, happy, and full of fun. One day, after we'd gotten our hair cut at Kenerson's, Dad said, "Let's go down to the train station and see what's going on."

That seemed odd. With only two trains a day, a freight at night and a passenger in the morning, there was never much going on at the Fryeburg station. We had a 1950 Studebaker at the time. Dad parked the Studie, and Ted and I followed him into the station. Except for the clerk behind the window, the place was empty. "When's the White Mountain Express arrive?" Dad asked the clerk.

The clerk looked up at the Regulator clock ticking away on the wall and said, "Ten-fifteen, same as always."

"Does it stop at North Conway?" Dad asked.

"Ayuh, ten-thirty-seven."

"How much for these two boys?"

"Quarter apiece."

Dad fumbled through his pockets and came out with a Walking Liberty fifty-cent piece. He slapped it on the counter, eagle-side up. "We'll take two."

I looked at Ted. Ted looked at me. Dad was going to put us on the train to North Conway.

The clerk handed Dad two tickets. "It's a nice ride through the valley," he said. "You gonna drive over and get 'em?"

"I'll be waiting for them," Dad said. "Come on, boys, you're going for a ride on the White Mountain Express." He gave us each a ticket and took us out to the platform to wait.

Ted was very excited. He jumped down onto the track and put an ear on a rail, listening for the train. It was a trick he'd seen on *Hopalong Cassidy*.

I was very nervous. I wasn't sure I wanted to go on the train without Dad. I stood on the platform begging Ted to get off the tracks, but Dad didn't seem to care. He sat down on a bench, lit up a Camel, and said to Ted, "Hear anything?"

"It's coming," Ted said, jumping up. A whistle blew and we could see a trail of smoke rising through the trees. There was another blast of the whistle and the big headlight of the White Mountain Express came steaming around the bend. I moved way to the back of the platform as the engine blew through the station like a summer storm, its bell clanging, smokestack puffing, and jets of white steam hissing from its wheels. The White Mountain Express ground to a stop, the couplings between the cars clinking and clanking as they readjusted their grips. The conductor lowered the stairs and stepped onto the platform. "Fryeburg! Fryeburg, Maine!" he bellowed.

"Let's go, boys," Dad said, grabbing my hand. He didn't have to grab Ted's. Ted had his ticket out and was ready to ride.

"Will you keep an eye on these boys for me?" Dad asked the conductor. The conductor adjusted his glasses and gave us the once-over. He looked hot in his blue serge uniform and woolen conductor's cap, especially next to Dad, who always wore a crisp white T-shirt and his old Navy khakis when we were in Maine. Dad looked cool.

"How far they going?"

"North Conway, but if I'm not there, I want to make sure they get off. I'm not chasing you to St. Johnsbury."

"Gonna try to beat us, are ya?"

"I'm going to give it a shot."

The conductor pulled a big gold watch out of his vest pocket. "Well, ya betta get a move on it. We'll be arriving at North Conway in eighteen minutes."

Dad didn't wait to see us go. He ran to the Studie, jumped in, and was off. "All aboard," the conductor yelled, and Ted and I scrambled up the steps. The smokestack chugged, our car rocked, the wheels squealed, and the White Mountain Express began to grind its way out of Fryeburg. Ted found us two seats by an open window, and we watched the back side of Fryeburg pass by. As the tracks started running parallel to Route 302, Ted yelled, "Look, there's Dad!"

Sure enough, there was Dad in the Studie, roaring along 302 and waving out the window. "Come on, Dad!" Ted yelled. He was so excited that everybody in our car, even the conductor, leaned out the windows and started cheering for Dad.

Whoooo, Whooo. We were coming to the crossing on 302. There was no gate, only a flashing light. Dad was passing cars like a madman. *Whooo, Whooo.* The puffs of smoke had turned into a steady stream as the train continued to pick up speed. "He's not gonna make it, not unless he can get by that hay truck," somebody yelled. Everybody agreed, except for Ted. "He'll make it," Ted proclaimed.

Dad must have seen an opening. The Studie swung out around the hay truck. Ted was standing up, pumping his arm, screaming, "Go Dad, go!" *Whooo, Whooo.* There was the crossing. I covered my eyes with my hands but peeked through my fingers. The lights started flashing. Dad wasn't going to make it. He'd have to stop. But the Studie didn't stop. It zipped over the tracks.

"Yeeay!" There was a big cheer as we scrambled to the other side of the car. There was Dad, buzzing along 302, his arm out the window giving the White Mountain Express a big wave. That was the last we saw of him. The train bridge over the Saco River was right after the tracks crossed 302. Cars had to go over the covered bridge another five miles down the road in Conway. Now the reality of being alone on the train to St. Johnsbury, Vermont, sank in. "Do you think Dad will be there?" I asked Ted.

"Don't worry, Davey," Ted said. "Dad'll be there."

And he was. When the train pulled into North Conway, there was Dad, leaning against the side of the Studie, smoking a Camel, reading the *Portland Press Herald*. The conductor put down the stairs and we jumped out. The other passengers were leaning out the windows laughing and yelling congratulations to Dad. "Where you guys been?" Dad said nonchalantly. "Seems like I've been waiting here half the day."

If nothing was better than going to Maine, nothing was worse than coming home. On the Friday night before we'd have to leave, the whole camp would have a cookout on the beach. The next morning, everybody would be busy packing. Reverend Jordan wanted us out by eleven so he'd have time to clean before the next wave of campers arrived that afternoon. Mom wanted to make sure that Little Beaver was spotless. She'd still be mopping the floors even after the car was packed. "Okay, boys, Mom wants you out of the cabin," Dad would say. "Why don't you take your last swim."

Ted and I would put on our suits—the leopard skins were just a one-year fad—and go down to the beach. We'd swim out to the raft and take a last look at the lake and the mountains. "Come on, Davey," Ted would say, "it's time to go." He knew if he didn't keep me moving, I'd start to cry. I'd dive into the water, watch the air bubbles stream through my fingers, and know that it would be the last time I'd see them for almost a year. Why did we have to go?

People would be moving from camp to camp hugging one

another and saying good-bye. They would look at me, see the sadness, and say, "It's okay, Davey. We'll be back next year." Then I would start to cry. Next year was too far away. Cars would begin to leave. I couldn't watch them, so I'd go sit in the woodshed by myself and sob harder with each parting honk. Finally, Mom would be ready to go and Ted would come get me. I'd climb into the back seat, my head down, tears dripping onto the pine pillow Dad had bought me at Solari's. Reverend Jordan would stick his head in the car window to say good-bye, but I'd be too sad to look up. "Put us down for Little Beaver the first two weeks of July," Dad would tell him.

"Ayuh," the Reverend would nod. "We won't open without ya." Then he'd look at me. "Davey sure does hate to leave," he'd say. "He'll be all right once you get on the road." But I never was. Crossing the line out of Maine was leaving everything I loved.

DAD'S HUMONGOUS PICKEREL

The same families came back to Jordan's every year, and they stayed in the same camps. We were in Little Beaver; the Garlands in Rose Marie; the Cunninghams in Loons Nest; the Dohertys in Arrowhead; the Raffertys, who were the Dohertys' cousins, in Snuggle Inn; the Largesses in Home; and the Bourneufs in Minn's Inn. We were like an extended family. We'd do everything together: go to church suppers, have cookouts on the beach, ride the Skimobile in North Conway, climb Pleasant Mountain in Bridgton, form a caravan and drive to St. Augustin de Woburn, the first town in Canada.

I'd usually wake up when I heard a screen door slam. Thanks to the old World War II blackout shades that Reverend Jordan used for drapes, my bedroom was always dark, but I could tell if the sun was out by looking at the pinholes in the shades. If little beams of light were poking through, it was going to be a nice day.

Ted and I would get up and do our chores while Mom cooked

a big breakfast on the woodstove: eggs, bacon, fried perch, home-made bread smeared with blueberry jam. Dad would be on the porch smoking a Camel, reading yesterday's paper. On the sill next to him, steam would be rising from a mug of coffee.

After breakfast, Ted and I would wander up to the swing between the two giant pines in front of Home Cottage. That's where the kids at Jordan's met to plan their day. There were about a dozen of us, and no one in a great hurry to do anything. While we were gathering, the Hood's diary truck would drive in and go from camp to camp delivering milk, eggs, and butter. After it came the Cushman's Bakery man. The sight of his black-and-white station wagon would start a race between Sister Cunningham and me. Sister was a little husky, like me, and we both wanted to be first in line to get the one box of choco-late doughnuts. For some reason, the Cushman's man never brought two.

If nothing else was going on, we might hitch a ride to town with whoever was going to Solari's to get the newspapers, the post office to mail some cards, or Oliver's Rexall Drugs to send a telegram. Mr. Oliver represented Western Union in Fryeburg. By midmorning, we'd all be at the beach swimming or boat-ing or lying on a towel soaking up the summer sun. By mid-afternoon, most of the camp would be at the beach, the men standing around in baggy bathing trunks, smoking Camels and talking about the Red Sox or how Ike was running the country, the women sitting around the picnic table in matronly, one-piece bathing suits, smoking Chesterfields and talking about shopping and where to get the best bargains. For the most part, we kids were ignored. As long as we showed up for meals, no-body seemed to care where we went or what we did, which was just fine with us.

•　　•　　•

Evenings at Jordan's were devoted to fishing. After supper, Dad would tell Ted and me to grab our poles and we'd head out. We always caught something. Lovewell Pond was loaded with hornpout, pickerel, and white and yellow perch, but everyone threw the yellows back. Local lore had it that yellow perch contained worms. When we were real little, Dad made our poles out of saplings and a piece of string with a hook tied on the end. He'd row us out to the raft, and that's where we'd fish. Unless we saw Old Tom.

Old Tom was the resident eagle. He had a nest somewhere on the back side of Arrowhead Mountain. From there, Tom could fish the ponds and lakes along the Fryeburg section of the Saco River. When we saw Old Tom dive for a fish, Dad would load us in the boat and row as hard as he could to the spot. If we got there in time, we'd get into a school of perch.

One evening while we were fishing on the raft, Old Tom surprised us by bursting out of a big pine on the shore right next to Jordan's. I'd never seen Old Tom that close. He was huge. He swooped down not thirty yards from us and came up with a fish. We could see the individual feathers on Tom's white head and tail, even the red blood running down the side of the fish, a nice white perch. "Get in the boat!" Dad yelled. Ted and I pulled in our lines and climbed into the boat while Dad stowed the anchor—a used paint can that Reverend Jordan had filled with cement—and grabbed the can of worms.

When we reached the spot, the water was silver with fish. "Quick, put your lines in!" Dad barked. He was clearly excited, and it took something to get Dad excited.

Bang. Bang. Bang. As soon as a worm was in the water, a fish would hit it. We'd pull the fish out and dangle it in front of Dad, waiting for him to take it off the hook. "Hurry up, Dad," we'd keep saying, "I need a new worm. I need a new worm." Dad couldn't bait the hooks fast enough. Fish were flopping all over the boat. I got so excited that once, by mistake, I threw my hook in without a worm. It didn't make any difference; the school was in a feeding frenzy. I pulled up the biggest fish of the night.

Suddenly, it was all over; the school moved on. When we counted up our catch, we'd landed thirty-three white perch in less than twenty minutes. The next day, Dad went to Oliver's and telegraphed the results to our hometown paper, the *Arlington Advocate*. Uncle Kirby mailed us a copy of the next edition. There on the sports page was a squib about our catch. It was the first time I'd ever seen my name in the paper.

There were a lot of good fishermen at Jordan's, but Mr. Garland was, without question, the best. Mr. Garland went out earlier than anybody else, came back later, and just about always caught more fish. For a great fisherman, Mr. Garland couldn't have been nicer. If you needed a bobber or lost your hook, you could row over to Mr. Garland's boat and he'd give you one. If you had a problem with your rod or reel, he'd fix it. You could ask Mr. Garland anything—where they were biting, what lures to use, how deep to set your hook—and, unlike some fishermen, he'd give you an honest answer.

Mr. and Mrs. Garland only had one child, Bobby, and Bobby could be a problem. He was always doing something to get attention. If you were swimming and got hit in the back of the head with a clump of wet sand, it was Bobby who threw it. If you were standing on the raft and somebody pushed you in from behind, it was Bobby who did it. If you were lying on the beach and somebody sneaked up and poured water on you, it was Bobby who'd be holding the pail laughing.

If Bobby really wanted attention, all he had to do was go fishing. Like Mr. Garland, Bobby was a super fisherman. The two of them would go out every night, and when they came in the whole camp would gather around to survey their catch. Watching the Garlands unload their boat was the highlight of an evening at Jordan's. The front of Mr. Garland's normally sparkling white T-shirt would be soiled from all the fish he'd held against his chest removing the hooks. There'd be fish everywhere: under the seats, wedged between the floorboards, hanging over the stern on a string.

"Here's a nice one," Mr. Garland would say, hoisting up a beautiful bass. "Bobby caught this one with a Hula Popper. Show them the Popper, Bobby." Half a dozen flashlights would focus first on the bass, then on the Popper. There'd be a chorus of *oohs* and *aahs*. Mr. Garland would point to the string and say, "Hand me that one, son," and a huge perch would flash in the lights. "There was a whole school of big ones like this baby over by Loon Island."

"Loon Island!" somebody would exclaim. Loon Island was on the other side of the lake. Nobody but Mr. Garland would row all the way over there looking for perch. One night the Garlands came in with an eel. Nobody could figure out what an eel was doing in Lovewell Pond, but if an eel was there, you could bet that the Garlands would catch it.

The Garlands stayed in Rose Marie Cottage. Mr. Doherty claimed that the reason the Garlands always reserved Rose Marie was because it was the camp nearest the main beach. "The Garlands don't want to strain their backs carrying all those fish," Mr. Doherty would scoff. He could joke about the Garlands because he was the only man at Jordan's who didn't fish. Catching and cleaning fish was not Mr. Doherty's idea of a good time. On his vacation he liked to play the ponies. While all the other men were getting into their boats, Mr. Doherty would get into his car and drive to Scarborough Downs with Joe Solari and his son, Louie. In addition to owning the general store, Joe and Louie owned a string of trotters. Black-and-white pictures of the

Solaris standing in the winner's circle with their horses lined the wall behind the soda fountain.

Like Rose Marie, Little Beaver was right on the water, but Little Beaver was about a hundred yards down the shore from the main beach. One reason Dad liked Little Beaver was because it had its own little sandy spot where we could land our boat. That meant when we came in from fishing, we didn't have to compete with the Garlands. Nobody wanted to compete with the Garlands.

Things got real bad in 1953 when the Garlands showed up with a brand-new three-horsepower Evinrude. That was the first outboard motor at Jordan's. Bobby had won it at the Sportsman's Show in Boston. Mr. Garland had entered Bobby in the casting contest, and Bobby had beaten everybody, even kids who were much older. Ted Williams had made the presentation. My brother Ted and I couldn't believe it when Dad showed us the picture in the February 16 *Boston Herald.* There was Bobby, standing between Mr. Garland and Ted Williams, holding the motor. At first I didn't recognize Mr. Garland in his coat and tie. Ted Williams had on a coat but no tie. Ted Williams never wore a tie. Bobby was in a plaid hunting shirt from Solari's. While Ted and I studied the picture, Dad shook his head and said, "It's going to be a long summer."

The Garlands' new mobility only added to their proficiency. They were coming in with bigger and bigger catches all the time. When Mr. Garland's brother, Dick, came for the Fourth of July, the Garlands tied a boat on top of Dick's car and headed for Kezar Lake. They were going after landlocked salmon. Nobody at Jordan's ever dreamed of catching a landlocked salmon.

That night, with the Garlands gone, Dad rowed our boat to the main beach. His normally sparkling white T-shirt had been soiled by a nice fourteen-inch white perch. For once, all the lights were focused on our fish. I went to bed happy, thinking Dad was the star. The next thing I knew, Ted was shaking me, "Get up, Davey. Get up," he was saying. "You've gotta see this fish!"

I stumbled into the kitchen, and there were Mr. Garland, his brother, Dick, and Bobby. Dick was holding the most beautiful fish I'd ever seen. It was a landlocked salmon, plump and silvery with green and pink speckles along its sides. The Garlands had caught it that night in Kezar and were going from cabin to cabin showing it off. Dad had been upstaged. His fourteen-inch white perch looked small and drab compared to the Garland's big, beautiful landlocked salmon.

At the Fourth of July cookout the next day, we had lots of peas and modest portions of perch. The Garlands' thick, rosy salmon steaks, slathered with butter and garnished with parsley, dominated the grill. They generously offered to share their salmon, but everyone except Mr. Doherty was too proud to accept. Mr. Doherty went back for seconds. "This is some fish," he said.

"There's a bigger one down in the weeds by the outlet," Mr. Garland said. "It's a humongous pickerel. I've seen it a couple of times, but I've never been able to hook it."

After the cookout, Dad began sleeping on the porch where there were no World War II shades to block out the light. I'd hear him get up with the sun, grab his fishing rod, and slip out the door. Dad took only one lure with him, a Johnson Weedless, so I knew where he was going. He was after that humongous pickerel.

On the third morning, I got up when I heard the screen door squeak and said, "Dad, can I come with you?"

"Sure," he said. "I could use some company."

While Dad rowed, I sat in the bow and gazed over his shoulder into the White Mountains. I could see a patch of snow still clinging to the top of Mount Washington. It was a glorious Maine morning, cool and clear without a breath of air. Lovewell Pond was totally calm. The arrow formed by the reflections of Pleasant and Arrowhead Mountains lay perfectly symmetrical along the far shore. High above, I saw Old Tom soaring on a thermal, his white head turning this way and that searching for a school of perch.

"There's Old Tom," I said.

"I see him," Dad said, but he kept rowing. Dad wasn't thinking about perch. He was totally focused on that humongous pickerel.

The sun was up over the trees when we passed Rappatuck, the other girls' camp on Lovewell Pond. Dad pulled out his handkerchief and wiped his brow. It was getting hot. We listened to a bugle playing reveille, and I squinted into the sun hoping to see some young, nubile campers sprinting for the showers. I thought about Janie Doherty, who was twelve and beginning to blossom, climbing up onto the raft, her suit being tugged down by the water. I was ten and beginning to notice these things, but as we glided by Rappatuck I wasn't offered so much as a glimpse. I hoped Dad's luck would be better than mine.

Dad let the boat come to rest in the middle of the lily pads, stowed the oars, and lit up a Camel. Dad smoked two packs of Camels a day. He'd get twenty cartons for a nickel a pack when he shipped out for his two weeks of active duty in the Naval Reserves. "Dad, when did you start smoking?" I asked him. If I was getting interested in girls, could cigarettes be far behind?

"During the Depression," he said, picking up his rod. "I started out smoking Benson & Hedges, but then Mr. Roosevelt gave me a job digging ditches for the WPA. All the guys would leave their cigarettes up on their dirt pile while they dug. When you walked along the ditch, it would be Camel, Camel, Camel, and then my Benson & Hedges. I didn't want to look like a sissy, so I switched to Camels." Dad snapped the Johnson Weedless onto the end of his leader and let it dangle over the side. The Weedless looked good even out of the water: a graceful silver spoon gleaming in the sunlight. "It's a dirty habit, Davey," Dad said, finishing his thought on smoking. "Don't you ever start."

"No, sir," I said, wondering what Dad thought about girls but not daring to ask.

Dad was a great caster. He had a strong arm. "Cracker" Keefe, who ran the newsstand in Arlington, used to say that if it hadn't been for the Depression, Dad could have played pro ball. Dad constantly reminded Ted and me that Ted Williams had developed his throwing arm from casting and that we should use the same motion. Ted Williams was our family idol; Ted was even named after him. Secretly, that was the thing that bothered us most about the Garlands' new motor. We didn't care that it gave them greater mobility. We were jealous that they'd had their picture taken with Ted Williams.

I watched with pride as the Weedless soared over the bog and plopped into the water a good thirty yards from our boat. Bobby Garland might be accurate, but he'd never have Dad's distance. I lay back in the warm sun as the Weedless snaked its way through the lily pads back to the boat. The key to a Weedless was the little bar on the underside that kept the hook from snagging. The bar was strong enough to resist the weeds, but it would depress and expose the hook when a fish bit the lure.

The problem was that Dad's old reel couldn't handle his powerful arm. Dad got a backlash on almost every cast. He was working on yet another bird's nest when I noticed that his line had gone taut. "Dad, you musta hooked a log," I said. That was not unusual. If a Weedless sank to the bottom, a twig could trip the bar.

"I'll worry about that after I get this line untangled,' Dad said, wedging the rod between his legs and lighting up another Camel.

Suddenly, I saw the end of the bog erupt. Lily pads exploded as the white underside of the biggest pickerel I'd ever seen twisted and turned over the surface. "Holy mackerel!" Dad shouted. "I've got 'im!" Ignoring the backlash, he started to reel in. I jumped up on the seat for a better look. He had him all right. The thrashing began moving toward the boat.

The next fifteen minutes were my father's finest. He stood erect, left foot propped against the gunwale, sweat pouring from his brow, muscles rippling under his sparkling white T-shirt, a Camel drooping from his mouth, playing that humongous pickerel for all it was worth. Even the Garlands had never brought home a fish this big. But this fish wasn't home yet. It was putting up a tremendous fight, giving Dad everything it had, tugging the Weedless all over the bog, using every trick in the book. Once, twice, three times it came totally out of the water, dancing on its tail. What a fish! Dad's old rod was nearly bent in half.

I was sure we were going to lose it when it went under the boat, but Dad scrambled to the stern and quickly guided the line around the keel with his free hand. That was it. The big fish seemed to acknowledge that it had been beaten. It floated slowly to the surface. I could see its whole body for the first time. It was at least a yard long.

Dad maneuvered the fish to the edge of the boat. "Okay, Davey," he said, "bring 'im in." We didn't have a net. With all the little stuff we caught, we'd never needed one. I leaned over, grabbed the line, and hoisted the fish. I could hear my father yelling, "Grab the leader! Grab the leader!" but he was too late. Just when I got the fish out of the water, it gave one last twitch. The line snapped, and the fish, all three feet of it, slid back into the water. It just lay there, its gills pumping for oxygen. The Weedless, the leader, and a couple of feet of line were dangling from its mouth. I stood there stunned, not knowing what to do, but Dad dropped his rod and lurched over the side, frantically plunging his arm into the water. "Grab the leader! Grab the leader!" he was still yelling, but he missed it. Dad's humongous pickerel flicked its tail and was gone forever.

It was a long, silent trip back to camp. I was still in the bow, so I couldn't see my father's face. I was surprised he didn't throw me overboard. Thank goodness we could sneak back to Little Beaver. I was so mortified that I didn't want to see any-body, and given the heat, I knew that the whole camp would be down at the main beach.

Unexpectedly, my father rowed right past Little Beaver. He beached our boat in front of Rose Marie. Everyone came over to see what we had caught. Mr. Doherty was just finishing a salmon croquette, compliments of Mrs. Garland. "Well, Jack, now that we've finally polished off the salmon, what have you got for us?" he said.

"We almost had that pickerel, but he was so big we decided we should leave him for the Garlands," Dad said.

Suddenly, I couldn't contain myself. I started to spit out the whole story. I was more excited than if we'd caught the fish. Mr. Garland wanted to know every detail: where we were, what type of lure we were using, how far Dad had cast, how the fish be-haved, how Dad kept him from getting tangled under the boat, how I grabbed the line and not the leader. By the time I got through, Mr. Garland was convinced that Dad had hooked the biggest fish in Lovewell Pond.

Dad just sat there, holding his rod, fingering the broken line. He didn't say a word. He didn't have to. He must have known that I'd sell his fish better than he could. And I did. For the rest of the summer, it didn't matter how many fish the Garlands brought in. All everyone wanted to know was whether they'd caught Dad's humongous pickerel.

JUST LOOKIN' FOR FISH

The Jordans stayed in Birch Knoll, a very rustic cabin back in the woods behind the main camp. It was Reverend Jordan, his wife, Ellen, and their two daughters, Mary and Sue, who gave Jordan's Camps its true Maine flavor.

Mary and Sue were about the same age as the rest of us, but they weren't like kids from Massachusetts. They had real thick Maine accents, never wore shoes, could run with the wind, and were the best swimmers in camp. Mary and Sue weren't afraid of anything. At night, after we'd come in from fishing, they'd take us to a haunted house down the shore from Jordan's. It was the scariest place I'd ever been. One night, a snake came out of a woodpile and wrapped itself around Mary's leg. When we saw the snake in the beam of the flashlight, we all screamed and ran away. Mary and Sue laughed. They thought it was funny. We'd follow Mary and Sue anywhere. They took us on hikes up Pleasant Mountain and down the outlet to a rope swing they knew about on the Saco River. The Jordan girls were Sacajaweas, leading the tenderfoots from Massachusetts through the wilds of Maine.

Mrs. Jordan was painfully shy. She was always working around the camp, painting, raking, and cleaning, but she seldom socialized with the other women. She was very kind to us kids. On rainy days, we'd all go to Birch Knoll and play long, heated games of Monopoly, listen to records on the Jordan's crank-up Victrola, and generally make nuisances of ourselves. Mrs. Jordan never seemed to mind. She'd bake batches of cookie, brownies, and muffins on the woodstove and let us eat as many as we wanted. Thanks to Mrs. Jordan, we never minded a rainy day.

Jack Jordan was a native of Fryeburg. He'd inherited the camps from his father and obviously loved them as much as we did. I had a hard time picturing Reverend Jordan as a minister. Every minister I'd ever seen wore black shoes, black pants, a black shirt, and a white collar. Whenever I saw Reverend Jordan, he was dressed in black high-top sneakers, khaki pants, and a white T-shirt. On weekends he'd go to his church in Saco, but during the week he'd be at the camps working: caulking boats, mending screens, fixing the pump, and doing the hundred other things it took to keep Jordan's running.

Reverend Jordan was always looking for things he could use to fix up the camps, but he never bought anything new. If it wasn't used, Jordan's Camps didn't need it. He'd often take me with him when he went scrounging. I loved these trips with the Reverend. We'd spend hours rummaging through old houses, barns, even the Fryeburg dump, looking for deals.

The Reverend knew everyone and was a skilled negotiator. He'd been a big track star at Fryeburg Academy, and he'd get talking about meets run long ago and who'd beaten whom, and eventually we'd get what we wanted at a good price. The guy who ran the dump had anchored the academy's relay team, so much of our time was spent at the dump swapping stories. The rerun of the 1930 upset of Gould Academy always resulted in a tour of the dump master's private collection, the junk he kept hidden behind his shed. Thanks to that upset of Gould, the Reverend picked up a lot of good stuff behind the shed.

One day while we were driving along, we passed a dead cat. "Uh-oh," the Reverend said. "We can't leave the poor fella like that." He stopped his little Nash and pulled a burlap bag out of the trunk. He carefully unfolded the bag and spread it out next to the cat. "Okay, Davey," he said. "You kick the cat while I hold the bag." I gave the cat a good boot, and in it went.

I didn't feel quite right about kicking an animal, even a dead cat, but it didn't bother the Reverend. He shook the cat to the bottom of the bag and twirled it around his head three times. "In the name of the Father" (*whoosh*), "the Son" (*whoosh*), "and the Holy Ghost" (*whoosh*). I watched in amazement as he let the bag go. The cat sailed through the woods to its final resting place. The Reverend stood respectfully until we heard a distant *thump,* then added an "Amen." When I told my father about the cat and the Reverend's benediction, he chuckled and said, "Jack Jordan's more Mainer than minister."

In 1955, the Reverend decided to move Jordan's Camps into the twentieth century when we found a bunch of used but perfectly serviceable flush toilets out behind the fairgrounds. The manager of the fairgrounds, a former sprinter for the academy, said that the Reverend was welcome to them. The Fryeburg Fair had gotten so big and successful that they'd just built a brand-new comfort station with all new toilets.

Everyone at camp was delighted. Block ice, woodstoves, and spring water were pleasant reminders of the past, but it was hard to get too nostalgic over a two-holer. But now that the Reverend had his toilets, how was he going to dig eight separate cesspools? These were the days before the Environmental Protection Agency, when a cesspool was just a hole in the ground reinforced by railroad ties. The easiest way would have been to hire a contractor with a backhoe to come in and dig the eight holes, but the Reverend couldn't afford a contractor, not when we campers were paying just twenty dollars a week. His solution was to take a sledgehammer and a crowbar and punch holes in the ground where he wanted the cesspools. Then, with all the kids in camp watching, he dropped nickels and dimes and at least one quarter per pool down the holes. We immediately started digging for the money. Within two days, the Reverend had his eight cesspools, and every kid in camp had unearthed enough change for a sundae at Solari's.

When the cesspools were done, the Reverend and I went to pick up the toilets in a logging truck he'd borrowed from a lumberjack who'd put the shot at the academy. We were cruising back to camp with our commodes when the Reverend said, "Davey, you seem awful quiet. Something wrong?"

I had to confess that there was. I'd been having an awkward summer. Over the Fourth of July, some friends of the Raffertys had come for a visit. They had a speedboat and water skis. They'd given each kid in camp three tries to get up. Ted, Bobby Garland, Richard Cunningham, Jimmy Doherty, Janie Doherty, and, of course, the Jordan girls all had made it. I hadn't. My arms weren't strong enough to lift my husky frame. That was pretty embarrassing. Then, on our annual trip to the Skimobile in North Conway, I'd had a hole in the bottom of my jeans. The Skimobile never stopped, so to get on, you had to run next to the little cars and slide onto your seat. The seats were made of wooden slats, and as I slid on, I didn't notice that one of the slats had slipped into the hole in my jeans. When I tried to get off, I couldn't. Before I could get my pants unstuck, I was in the wheelhouse making a U-turn. Gears were grinding, cables were squeaking, and I was screaming that I wanted off. When I came out, all the kids from camp were standing on the platform laughing. Even the guy who was supposed to be helping people was laughing. He told me I couldn't get off from that side. I'd have to ride down to the bottom and come up again. That was even more embarrassing.

The water skis and the Skimobile were only part of it. My biggest problem was that I was twelve, we were about to finish another year at camp, and I had never caught a bass. Nobody had ever come out and said it, but everyone knew you weren't a man at Jordan's until you'd caught a bass. Richard Cunningham, who was fourteen, had just landed his first, which was okay, but then Brian Doherty, who was only nine, had come in the night before with a nice two-pounder. Now Brian was strutting around camp, bragging about his bass. That was *really* embarrassing.

To make matters worse, I'd hooked a beauty the previous week and lost it. I'd been fishing with Jimmy Doherty, Brian's older brother, out at the Ledge. The Ledge was a pile of big rocks under the water over by Loon Island, and while Lovewell Pond wasn't noted for bass, if you knew what you were doing and got lucky, you just might hook a bass at the Ledge.

It had been a classic Maine evening. The sun had just set behind the White Mountains. The water was calm as a millpond. I was using a brand-new Jitterbug that I'd gotten at Solari's. Mr. Garland had told me that bass loved Jitterbugs because, coming across the water, they looked and sounded like a wounded frog. I'd made a perfect cast and the Jitterbug was *plop, plop, plop*-ing its way back to the boat like a wounded frog.

Wham! My rod bent in half. I'd never felt anything like it. Hooking a bass was nothing like hooking a perch, or even a pickerel. Perch nibble, pickerel bite, bass devour. The Jitterbug was gone, but not for long. A moment later, a huge bass came sailing out of the water, shaking its head, trying to throw the hook. "Wow," I screamed, "I got 'im."

"Keep your rod up," Jimmy said, quickly reeling in his own line. "Don't give him any slack." If you had slack in your line, a bass would use it to throw the hook. At least, that's what everyone said. The bass went down again. "Watch it, Davey," Jimmy said. "He's heading for the rocks." The rocks were bad. If a bass got into them, he'd cut your line. I gave my line a good jerk. *Snap.* The rod went straight. There was nothing on the other end. My bass was gone.

To add insult to injury, he'd taken my new Jitterbug with him. But that wasn't the end of it. Bobby Garland caught my bass two nights later. It still had my Jitterbug in its mouth. The whole camp got a big chuckle when Bobby reached into the bottom of the boat, held up the bass, and presented me with my lure. "Here you go, Davey," he said. "Try not to lose it again. Har, har."

After hearing my story about the bass, the Reverend told me to relax. "Don't worry, Davey," he said. "I'll take you out tonight and we'll catch you a bass. Ayuh."

I was very excited. No one had ever seen the Reverend fish, but everyone knew he was a great sportsman. There were three huge bass mounted on the wall of Birch Knoll, and they all were bigger than anything the Garlands had ever caught. When we asked Mrs. Jordan where they'd come from, she'd said, "Jack got 'em all out of the pond."

Right after supper, I grabbed my rod and went down to sit by the Reverend's boat. I waited and waited. All the other boats went out, but still there was no sign of the Reverend. The sun had almost set before he arrived. He was carrying a big army-surplus flashlight and a used coffee can. "Y'all set, Davey?"

"Yessir."

"Well, push 'er out, and we'll get ya your bass."

Some of the boats were already coming in as we rowed toward the Ledge. The Reverend rowed the way he must have run. He had a strong, easy, athletic stroke. When I closed my eyes, I felt as though I was in a motorboat. It was almost dark when we reached the shiny tin can that marked the Ledge. I grabbed the anchor and prepared to drop it, but the Reverend said, "Not yet, Davey." He squinted through his wire-rimmed glasses and carefully lined us up with a tall pine that stood silhouetted above the tree line. When he felt that he had us in exactly the right spot, he said, "Okay, Davey, put 'er down."

The Reverend reached into the coffee can and brought out the biggest night crawler I'd ever seen. He fondled it in his hand and appeared to be tickling its belly. "Ayuh, he's ready," he said. "Pass me your hook." I watched as the Reverend carefully wound the hook through the worm. When he was finished, he said, "Drop 'im in. Give 'im about eight feet."

I did as instructed. By now it was totally dark. The sudden light took me by surprise. The Reverend was shining the big army-surplus flashlight down the line into the water. I thought this was very strange. "What are you doing, Reverend Jordan?"

He kept staring into the water. "Oh, nawthin'. Just lookin' for fish."

Before I had a chance to say anything else, there was a strong jerk on the line and my rod bent. I don't remember the actual fight, but it didn't last very long. The next thing I knew, the Reverend had grabbed the leader and was pulling my bass into the boat. "Ayuh. Ain't the biggest fish in the pond, but it'll do," he said. I had to agree. This little fellow would never claim a spot on the Reverend's wall, but it was my first bass.

The whole camp was waiting for us when we rowed in. There was a big cheer as I proudly held up my bass. At last, I was feeling pretty good about myself. Later, back at Little Beaver, we were sitting on the porch and I was telling Dad how the Reverend used the flashlight to look for fish. Dad chuckled and said, "We'd better keep that to ourselves."

"Why?" I said.

"We don't want to give away any of the Reverend's secrets."

It took me a few years to fully appreciate what the Reverend had done. Jacking fish, even to repair the pride of a twelve-year-old kid, is not universally accepted as sporting, but Dad was right: Jack Jordan was more Mainer than minister, and I for one am glad of it.

THE GOOD SAMARITAN

Each year, more and more outboard motors were showing up at Jordan's. In addition to the Garland's three-horsepower Evinrude, Mr. Largess had a half-horsepower putt-putt that gave him all the speed he needed for trolling, the Bourneufs had a three-horsepower Johnson, and in the summer of '55 the Dohertys arrived with a brand-new five-horsepower Elgin. Mr. Doherty got Reverend Jordan to assign Arrowhead an almost new Lone Star aluminum boat that the Reverend had gotten a deal on someplace. Putting the Elgin on the Lone Star meant the Dohertys had the fastest rig at Jordan's. Be it horses or boats, Mr. Doherty liked speed.

That winter, Dad decided we should get an outboard. He'd seen a three-horsepower Evinrude for $150 at Corsi's Marina in Arlington. "If it's good enough for Ted Williams," he said, "it's good enough for us." Plus, Dad figured if anything ever went wrong with the motor, Mr. Garland could fix it. Ted and I were elated. The flies at the spring weren't nearly as annoying as

Bobby Garland, Peter Bourneuf, and now Jimmy Doherty buzzing around us in their outboards.

"Boys," Dad told us, "I'll put up seventy-five dollars if you can earn the other seventy-five. Ted, I figure you can make fifty caddying, and Davey, you should be able to make twenty-five by getting a paper route."

Ike was leading the country through a postwar boom, and Dad was feeling better about money. We'd put in a new kitchen, traded the Studie for a '55 Ford Country Squire, and started going to Jordan's for three weeks every year rather than two. Now Dad was going to put up half the money for an outboard motor if Ted and I could earn the other half. "We can do it," Ted said.

All that spring, I delivered the *Boston Herald* for $1.75 a week while Ted caddied at the Winchester Country Club. On the last Thursday in June, Dad took us down to Corsi's Marina and gave Mr. Corsi the cigar box containing our savings. Mr. Corsi emptied the nickels, dimes, quarters, and dollars onto his glass counter and added them up. "Seventy-five to the penny," he said. Dad gave him a check for the other seventy-five and we had our motor. Watching Mr. Corsi load the shiny new Evinrude into the back of Dad's '55 Country Squire was one of my proudest moments. Ted and I had earned it, or at least half of it.

With the motor, we needed the extra week at Jordan's. Now we could fish all of Lovewell Pond—the Ledge, Loon Island, the back side of Pine Island, the outlet, the inlet, the bog—but having the extra week caused a dilemma for Dad. The Maine Department of Inland Fisheries and Game offered two types of adult nonresident fishing licenses, one for fourteen days and the other for the whole season. The fourteen-day license cost six dollars, but the whole season was fifteen. Nine bucks was a lot of money in the mid-fifties, especially for the campers at Jordan's. Mr. Garland bought a license for the full season, but the other adults chose to sit on the beach and watch the kids, and for good reason. Getting caught without a fishing license was expensive. Viola Cunningham had found that out the previous year.

The Cunninghams were from Beverly, Massachusetts. Langdon Cunningham worked for United Shoe and was a deacon at Beverly's Dane Street Congregational Church. It was a position he held with great pride, so around Jordan's, Mr. Cunningham was known as the Deacon. The Deacon was by far the best horseshoe player at Jordan's, but he wasn't much of a fisherman. It was Mrs. Cunningham who liked to fish. Every night, right after dinner, the Deacon would tuck Viola into the stern of one of the old wooden boats and row her to Lucky Rock, a huge boulder just down the shore from Jordan's. Lucky Rock was the only place the Cunninghams ever fished, and since it was an easy row, the Deacon saw no need for a motor.

The game warden showed up once a summer. He'd come down the airport road and launch his boat at the west end of the lake. The warden had a ten-horsepower Johnson, and it was tough to outrun him. Some tried it, but not the Cunninghams. He caught them at Lucky Rock. It was the first summer the Cunninghams had stayed at Jordan's for three weeks, and they didn't realize that Mrs. Cunningham's license had expired. Naively, they pleaded ignorance, but the warden was unmoved. The next day, Mrs. Cunningham had to appear in Oxford County District Court. The Deacon nearly fainted when the judge fined her thirty-five dollars. That was a full week's rent at Jordan's. And that wasn't the worst of it; the following week Viola Cunningham of Beverly, Massachusetts, was listed for fishing without a license on the police blotter in *The Bridgton News*. The Deacon was mortified.

"I'm only going to buy a fourteen-day license," Dad told Mom as we zipped through the Ossipees on the way to Jordan's. "The boys' junior licenses are only two twenty-five, and they're good for the season. I'll watch them for a few days at the beginning and end, and save nine bucks. Two weeks' fishing is plenty for me."

It was a good plan, only it didn't work. Dad did all right for the first couple of days. He sat on the beach and watched Ted and me fish the whole lake with the Evinrude. We were drawing a crowd almost as big as the Garlands' when we came in. On the third night, Dad decided he'd come with us. "I'll run the motor while you guys troll," he said. We could have done it by ourselves, but having Dad along would be okay. After all, half the motor was his.

We were trolling past Lucky Rock when we saw Old Tom dive into a school of perch. He was a good quarter mile away, but that was no problem. "Reel in!" Dad yelled, giving the Evinrude the gas.

It was a big school of white perch, the likes of which we hadn't seen for some time. Ted and I started pulling in some beauties. Watching was too much for Dad. "Davey," he said, "let me see your rod. I want to make sure you have enough play."

I must have had plenty of play, because Dad landed a beauty, and then another, and another. When I asked for my rod back, he turned to Ted. "Ted, let me test yours for a minute."

Dad was weaving a fat, juicy worm onto Ted's hook when a boat pulled up next to us. We'd been so busy fishing that we hadn't seen it coming, but I recognized it. The boat was powered by a big twenty-five-horsepower Mercury and belonged to a guy down at the west end of the lake.

"You fellas got your licenses?" the guy asked. "The warden just put in."

"Thanks," Dad said.

The guy gunned the Merc and sped down to Lucky Rock to warn the Cunninghams.

"Let's head in," Dad said, stowing Ted's rod.

"But Dad," Ted protested, pointing to the fish jumping all around us. "We've got our licenses, and look at all the fish."

"The warden scans the lake with binoculars before he comes out," Dad said, priming the motor. "He might have seen me fishing. And after what happened to Viola, I'm not taking any chances."

Dad opened up the Evinrude and made a beeline for the camps. We waved as we went by the Cunninghams. The Deacon stopped rowing, reached into the bottom of the boat, and held up a big fish in each hand. He wasn't worried about the warden. This year, the Cunninghams knew they were legal.

We could see the warden with his ten-horsepower Johnson checking a boat at the Ledge. He'd be coming our way next. Dad fiddled with the mixture, trying to coax more speed out of the Evinrude. Our three little horses surged ahead. You couldn't beat an Evinrude. Ted Williams gave only the best.

"When we land," Dad said, keeping his voice low so it wouldn't carry over the water, "I'm going to take the rods and run up to the cabin. You boys unload the fish." Dad was out of the boat and into Little Beaver in no time.

"If the warden comes in and checks us," Ted told me, "I'll do the talking, but if he asks you, these are all our fish." Thankfully, the warden didn't come in. He stopped to check the Cunninghams at Lucky Rock, then zoomed across the lake. We brought the fish up to the camp and walked down to the main beach with Dad. Reverend Jordan was there raking. "In early," he said. "Thought they'd be bitin' tonight."

"They were," Dad said. "The boys got into a nice school of perch, but the guy with the Mercury down at the west end came by and told us the warden was out. I haven't gotten my license yet so I decided to come in."

"The good Samaritan, eh?" the Reverend said. "Better watch out. Warden finds somebody's goin' around warnin' people, he's not gonna like it."

"Well, I hope he doesn't find out," Dad said. "The guy did me a favor."

The Reverend scanned the lake looking for the warden. "Uh-oh," he said. "Doesn't look good."

Across the lake, we could see the warden's boat pulled up next to the good Samaritan. While we were watching, the Cunninghams rowed in. The Deacon was all smiles. He held up a string of big fish. "Lucky Rock was lucky tonight," he said.

"We can see that," Dad said, admiring the fish. "Did you get checked by the warden?"

"You know, that was the strangest thing," the Deacon said. "We got checked twice."

"Twice?" Dad said.

"Yes," the Deacon said, scratching his head. "First the warden with the Mercury came by, then Ervin Lord, the one with the Johnson. I'll never forget *him*. It was Ervin Lord who gave us the ticket last year. I let him know we didn't appreciate being checked twice. I told him with all the money they make in fines, it's no wonder the state can afford two wardens."

The Deacon had no idea what he'd done, and neither Dad nor Reverend Jordan told him. According to the following week's police blotter, the judge fined the good Samaritan fifty dollars for obstructing justice. After Dad read it, he put down *The Bridgton News* and said to Ted and me, "Boys, I'm glad we got the Evinrude. I think it just saved us some money."

GETTING HOOKED

Aunt Lil was my father's younger sister. Based on the rave reviews we gave Jordan's, she and Uncle Jim and their two girls, Sandra and Heidi, rented a camp one year, but Jordan's wasn't their cup of tea. Uncle Jim was a sailor, not a fisherman, and Aunt Lil was a bit of a swell. To her, there was nothing quaint about cooking over a woodstove, using blocks of ice for refrigeration, or going to a spring for water. And I couldn't begin to imagine Aunt Lil sitting on a two-holer.

Before the Great Depression, Dad's family had some money, and even though it was long gone, Aunt Lil still tried to maintain what she perceived to be the Morines' social standing. Sandra and Heidi, who were the same age as the Jordan girls, were being groomed to become debutantes. They were never allowed to go barefoot and were discouraged from socializing with people who did. Two weeks at Jordan's was more than enough for Aunt Lil. In the summerof '52, she and Uncle Jim rented a cottage on the Upper Bay of Kezar Lake. When they invited us up for a visit, Dad didn't want to go. He didn't want to give up a day of his vacation at Jordan's. Mom said we had to go. She even made Ted and me wear our church clothes. There would be no jeans and T-shirts visiting Aunt Lil at Kezar Lake.

Aunt Lil and Uncle Jim were staying at a resort called Hewn Oaks. Hewn Oaks was nothing like Jordan's Camps. It sat high on a hill looking west over the lake into the White Mountains. The cottages (they definitely were not camps) had electric stoves, electric refrigerators, running water, and, of course, indoor plumbing. With all these amenities, Uncle Jim had to be paying a bundle, but Uncle Jim could afford it. He was an up-and-coming engineer at Lever Brothers, and according to Dad, Uncle Jim was "doing real well." Even I could see that. Uncle Jim drove a big new Lincoln and had bought himself a big new sailboat.

While Aunt Lil, Sandra, and Heidi prepared lunch, Uncle Jim took Dad, Mom, Ted, and me out in his boat. As we tacked back and forth across the Upper and Middle Bays of Kezar, Uncle Jim pointed out the grand camps that made the lake so exclusive. "There's Westways," he said, pointing the stem of his pipe at a fancy boathouse and large lodge overlooking the Upper Bay. "It belongs to William Armstrong Fairburn, the president of Diamond Match."

I knew Diamond Match. We used Diamond matches to light the stove at Jordan's, and Diamond Match owned the mill in Fryeburg. "See that tree house?" Uncle Jim said, once again pointing his pipe. "That's where Rudy Vallee used to bring his showgirls." Uncle Jim winked at my father. "Rumor has it he wouldn't let them down until they'd given him a favor."

Eventually, we sailed past the most beautiful camp I'd ever seen. The pines were tall and straight, the grass a luxurious green, the beach meticulously raked, with all the chairs freshly painted and set in a line. Brown cottages that looked like Swiss chalets were set discreetly among the pines. Orange lanterns hung along the neatly trimmed paths. As we got closer, I could see that a black goose flying through a full moon was stenciled on each lantern.

"That's Severance Lodge," Uncle Jim said proudly, "the jewel in Kezar's crown." I'd heard of Severance Lodge. It was right opposite Severance Lodge that the Garlands had caught their salmon.

At Jordan's, when somebody came for lunch, we cooked red hot dogs down on the beach. At Hewn Oaks, Aunt Lil served cucumber sandwiches with the crusts cut off out on the veranda. Dad, Ted, and I couldn't wait to get back to Lovewell Pond. Mom never wanted to leave. She'd fallen in love with Kezar.

After our visit to Uncle Jim and Aunt Lil's, Mom set aside one day each summer for a tour of Kezar Lake. Ted and I would beg to stay back at Jordan's, but our protests were in vain. "I don't ask for much," Mom would say. "This is one thing you can do for me." She was right and we knew it. For the most part, Mom let us do whatever we wanted in Maine.

Our annual tour of Kezar was always the same. We'd go to the Kezar Lake Marina and Dad would rent a little boat with a three-horsepower motor from Mr. Perry, the owner. We'd pile in and spend the day puttering around the Upper and Middle Bays looking at the grand camps and bobbing in the wakes of their owners' big, spiffy mahogany inboards. Before we could go back to Jordan's, Mom would make Dad stop at the office of William E. Severance, Realtor. The office of William E. Severance, Realtor, was in a beautiful white Cape with black trim right in the center of Lovell. It commanded a spectacular view of the entire Presidential Range and set the tone for exclusivity, which is what William E. Severance, Realtor, was selling.

During the fifties and sixties, William E. Severance and his brother Harold controlled Kezar Lake. Harold owned Severance Lodge and Bill held every exclusive listing on the lake. The Severance brothers were from Massachusetts originally, and Bill Severance had some connection with Arlington, which probably was why he was so nice to Mom. He had to have known that we couldn't afford anything on Kezar. Our Studebaker was a dead giveaway. People on Kezar drove Cadillacs.

Each year, our tour of Kezar got more and more frustrating as the list of properties Mom "could have had" grew longer and longer. "Jack, we could have bought that place for three thousand," she'd say as we motored past a little camp down in the marsh by the Narrows. "Bill Severance just sold it for ten."

Dad would ignore her. He'd made it clear from the beginning that he wasn't interested in owning a summer home. "Donna, how many times do I have to tell you," he'd say, "I don't want the maintenance and we can't afford the expense. Let Jack Jordan fix the screens and pay the taxes. When I come to Maine, I'm not worrying about those things. I just want to relax."

When Mom came out of Bill Severance's office, she usually was wringing her hands over another deal she'd missed. In the summer of '64, she emerged excited. "Mr. Severance has some lots he wants to show us," she said. "It's a new development called Ladies Delight. It's on the Lower Bay." Dad rolled his eyes. Ted and I rolled our eyes. Here were more properties we could add to Mom's list of missed opportunities. "They all have water frontage," she continued, "and the prices start at fifteen hundred."

Fifteen hundred on Kezar? Impossible! Mom handed us the price list. Sure enough, the lots on Ladies Delight ranged from $1,500 to $3,500. "I guess it won't hurt to have a look," Dad said.

Kezar is a long, thin lake that runs nine miles north to south. The Upper and Middle Bays cover the first five. Then there's a mile-long corridor of mostly marshland. This corridor is more of a river than a lake. It could be the outlet for Kezar, only it opens up onto the Lower Bay. Physically, socially, and economically, the Lower Bay is a separate lake. It's like the Harvard summer school. Going to the summer school is not really going to Harvard, and being on the Lower Bay is not really being on Kezar— but it's close.

We followed Mr. Severance's big Cadillac over the Narrows and turned onto a dirt road that had been freshly graded. The road went through a field, then up a hill into a tunnel of towering pines. At the bottom of the hill, the road T-ed at the lake. Mr. Severance stopped his Caddie and got out. He was a wizened little man who played his cards close to his chest. Certain listings were for certain people, and he was careful whom he let on the lake and where.

"This is Ladies Delight," Mr. Severance said, pointing up and down the road. "Road runs for about a mile. Sixty lots. Numbers are on the trees. Stakes mark the boundaries. Forty-three already sold. The list tells which lots are still available." Mr. Severance stopped and rubbed his chin, as if thinking to himself. "Very popular. Suspect they'll all be gone in a couple of weeks. Look 'em over. See one you like, I'll be back at the office. This would be a good place for you."

We spent the next two hours walking up and down Ladies Delight looking at lots. Dad seemed to be taking the search seriously. With Ted out of college and me halfway through, he didn't seem to be constantly worried about money. Plus, Mom had finally found something we could afford. I liked finding the stakes, checking out the frontage, evaluating the views, weighing the pros and cons of each lot. It was exciting. Mom, of course, was most interested in lots that already had been sold. She wanted to see what she'd missed. That had been her modus operandi over the last fifteen years. Dad finally turned her around. "Dammit, Donna, stop looking at the ones already sold and pick one that's not." Dad had decided to buy a lot.

With Dad's approval, our search turned serious. Mom finally narrowed her choice down to #56. This lot had the best view on Ladies Delight, if not the whole lake, but there were two obvious problems. First was the size. It was the smallest lot on Ladies Delight. Most lots averaged 100 feet of shore frontage by 200 feet in depth, but #56 fronted on a little cove and was barely 120 feet deep. Second was the old trailer next door. There was a restriction in the Ladies Delight subdivision plan that prohibited trailers, but this trailer wasn't part of the subdivision. It had been there for years.

Mom began to waver. She didn't come to Kezar to be next to a trailer. She went back and looked at some of the other lots. None of them had the view of #56, and they all were more expensive. "If you like the view, get fifty-six," Dad told her. "That trailer won't be there forever."

Mom returned to #56 for another look. She walked down to the shore, climbed up on a big rock, and stared at the mountains. "I can see Mount Washington!" she exclaimed. "I feel like I'm in Switzerland." Mom had never been to Switzerland, but that didn't matter. We were going to buy #56. A thrill swept over me as I watched Mom and Dad sign the papers back at Mr. Severance's office. I liked buying real estate.

When I graduated from college two years later, Dad gave me $3,000 that my grandfather had left me. Dad had been saving it to pay for college, but I'd made it through without having to dip into it. He assumed I'd use the money for graduate school, and so did I until Mom and I made her annual stop at William E. Severance's. Since Dad had bought the lot, he no longer had to make the trip. He and my little brother, Bill, stayed at Jordan's and went fishing. I went with Mom because Pete Wylie, a friend of mine who had a pickup, was coming for the weekend to help me clear some brush from Mom's lot. I needed her blessing on what we were going to remove. To Mom, lot #56 was sacred.

Rather than wait in the car, I went in to see Mr. Severance with Mom. Now that I was out of college, I was thinking I might want to work in real estate. During our visit, I asked Mr. Severance if there were any lots left on Ladies Delight. "No, you were lucky to buy when you did," he said, then added, "but I do have some land for sale on Horseshoe Pond. It's just behind Kezar. Small but very private. Good fishing back there."

Mr. Severance went to his files and pulled out a plat of the subdivision on Horseshoe Pond. "Here you go," he said, spreading the plat out on his big pine table. "Twelve lots." He pointed at the map. "Right here, on the inside of the Frog." Horseshoe Pond, as the name indicated, was shaped like a horseshoe. The Frog was the wedge of land in the middle, so named for the wedge-shaped prominence in the sole of a horse's hoof. "Just went on the market," Mr. Severance said, rubbing his chin. "Ten dollars a front foot. At that price, they'll move pretty fast."

"I'd like to take a look at them sometime," I said. "How do you get to Horseshoe Pond?"

Mr. Severance showed me a map and gave me a list of the lots and the prices. The next day, after we'd finished with Mom's lot, I told Pete to pull into the marina. "There're some lots on a back pond I want see," I said, "but I think we're going to need a canoe to get a good look at them."

Even though the road to Horseshoe Pond was owned by the town, it was barely passable. As we bounced over rocks and through gullies, I could see why the pond was "very private." Even Ebenezer Kezar, the trapper who first explored the Saco River Valley, would have had trouble finding it. After what seemed like ten miles but was more like two, Pete stopped the pickup on the top of a small wooden dam. To the left was Horseshoe Pond, to the right, Sucker Brook. "Where the hell are we?" he said.

We pulled the pickup into a small clearing with a hand-painted sign that read "Town Landing." We got out and launched the canoe. Pete and I paddled up one side of the Frog, then down the other. Except for a couple of deserted fish camps and one unobtrusive little cabin at the far end of the horseshoe, the pond was totally deserted. Signs along the west shore indicated that part of it was in the White Mountain National Forest. We stopped at a small sandy beach, stripped down, and went for a swim. The water was crystal clear and the pond deep. "This place is a little jewel," Pete said. I agreed.

After our swim, we began evaluating the lots that were for sale. They started at the town landing and followed an old logging road that ran up the west side of the Frog. The last three lots, the ones farthest from the town landing, were the nicest. They totaled 335 feet of frontage, $3,350, and I wanted them.

As we paddled back to the landing, I could hear voices in the woods. People were walking along the road checking out the lots. Soon, they'd be coming to my three. I started paddling harder. When we got to the landing, there were two cars with Massachusetts plates parked next to Pete's pickup. "Let's go," I said. We threw the canoe in the back of truck and headed for Mr. Severance's office.

I pulled out the plat and showed him the three lots I wanted. He pulled out a calculator and punched in some numbers. "That'll be three thousand three hundred and fifty dollars," he said.

I screwed up my courage. "Would you take three thousand? It's all I've got."

There was a long silence as Mr. Severance rubbed his chin. "Ayuh," he finally said, "I can do that."

The same thrill swept over me as when I'd watched Mom and Dad buy their lot. I tried to act as if spending my total inheritance was something I did every day, but Mr. Severance must have seen my hand shaking as I signed the purchase and sale agreement. "That's a good buy," he said, as if to calm me. "You won't lose anything on those lots."

My father didn't think it was such a good buy. He couldn't believe I'd spent all of Grampa's money on three lots on a pond somewhere in Lovell. "There isn't any power back there," he said. "Who'd ever want them? And what about graduate school?"

"Don't worry," I told him. "I'm going to business school. I want to learn everything I can about real estate."

Two summers later, I'd finished my first year of business school at the University of Virginia and was spending a weekend with Mom, Dad, and Bill at Jordan's. While Dad and Bill fished, Mom and I drove up to Lovell to look at our lots. When we stopped at William E. Severance's, Mr. Severance showed us a listing he had for a cabin on Ladies Delight. Mom and I went down to look at it. The cabin was right at the start of the Narrows, at the other end of the road from Mom's lot. It didn't have Mom's view and the cabin wasn't much nicer than Little Beaver, but it was on Kezar, and that made all the difference. Location, location, location. That's what I'd learned at business school.

"I'm going to buy it," I told Mom.

"How?" she said.

"OPM," I said. "Other people's money." That was another thing I'd learned in business school. The idea was to borrow OPM and leverage the hell out of it, so that's what I did. The cabin was listed for $14,000. I offered Mr. Severance $13,000. When that was accepted, I borrowed $4,000 from the student loan fund for the down payment and took a fifteen-year mortgage for $9,000 at 7 percent from the Norway Savings Bank. Then I started renting out the cabin for $125 a week.

It had been twenty years since we'd visited Aunt Lil and Uncle Jim at Hewn Oaks. Now everything I had, and then some, was invested in or around Kezar Lake. I was hooked on real estate.

THE RUDY VALLEE DEFENSE

On June 5, 1969, I proposed to Ruth Arthur Sisler. We were on the porch of my cabin watching the sunset. Ruth Arthur Sisler was from New Jersey and had never been to Maine, at least my Maine. She was so smitten by the lake, the mountains, and my little summer home that she accepted immediately. As an engagement present, I bought Ruth a used canoe from the Kezar Lake Marina. Mr. Perry, who owned the marina, was selling out, and I was able to negotiate the price down from $125 to $110. Reverend Jordan would have been proud of me. Dad was. He was so pleased I'd proposed to Ruth, he christened the canoe the *Ruda.*

I'd just graduated from business school and was going to work in New York City negotiating parking-lot leases for Hertz. Ruth had just graduated from college and had taken a merchandising job in New York. I knew that living in the city was going to be expensive and that money would be tight. I didn't tell Ruth, but I was worried that I might be carrying too much debt.

In addition to our normal living expenses, I had to start paying back all my student loans, and I owed Norway Savings Bank $80.90 every month for the cabin. I'd left us no margin for error.

I'd been able to rent out the cabin for most of the summer. Dad had taken it for the first three weeks in July. He still liked the long days for fishing and was eager to try his luck on Kezar. He'd never forgotten the Garlands walking into Little Beaver with that beautiful salmon. Mom was just happy to be within walking distance of her lot. For her, moving up to Kezar was a long-held dream come true.

I was delighted when Dad told me that I could have the cabin over the Fourth of July. Ted had really crossed the line when he'd married a girl from Maine, and Dad, Mom, and Bill were going over to the coast to spend the weekend with Ted's in-laws. Having the cabin for a holiday weekend was an offer I couldn't refuse. I'd started my job with Hertz on June 16 and was already sick of the Big Apple. Ruth was living at home with her family in New Jersey until we were married. I'd gotten a sublet for the summer and was spending my nights tromping around the hot, dirty, smelly streets of Manhattan trying to find us a permanent apartment. On the weekends, I'd take a bus out to New Jersey and stay with Ruth and her family, but that meant Ruth and I never had any time alone. We needed to get back to Maine.

The problem was getting there. I couldn't afford to keep a car in the city, and I didn't want to ask Ruth's parents if I could borrow one. They were not pleased with the prospect of Ruth going to Maine for the Fourth of July. It would be the first time in her life that Ruth hadn't spent the Fourth with them at the Jersey Shore. "Why would you ever want to go to Maine when you could go to the Shore?" Ruth's mother asked me.

"Because I have a cabin in Maine," I told her.

"Well, you should sell it and get a place at the Shore," she said. I didn't try to tell her that Maine was about ten times more beautiful. Nobody was ever going to convince Ruth's mother that the sun didn't rise and set over the Jersey Shore.

I called Clark Smyth. Clark was good friend from business school. He and his wife, Sally, had just moved to the city. I knew Clark would like Kezar; he was an avid sportsman who liked anything having to do with the out-of-doors. Clark's '62 Volkswagen bus was always filled with his toys. There were golf clubs, softball gloves, his special bat, fishing rods, a mask, fins, his special tennis racquet, badminton racquets, a surfboard. The back of Clark's bus looked like a sporting goods store.

"Clark, do have the bus with you?" I said.

"Sure," he said, sounding surprised that I'd even ask. "That's where I keep all my stuff."

"Do you think it can make it to Maine?"

"No problem. When do you want to go?"

"Fourth of July weekend. I have to work Thursday, but we can leave first thing Friday morning."

"Sounds good to me."

We chugged across the Triborough Bridge at 9:00 A.M. on Friday, the Fourth of July. The bus didn't break any speed records, but by 5:30 P.M. we were watching Mr. Craig custom-cut four juicy T-bone steaks at the Lovell Country Store. While Ruth and Sally finished the shopping, Clark and I rummaged through the cooler for a couple of cold Narragansetts. We were set for the weekend.

As Clark guided the bus through the towering white pines that lined the road to Ladies Delight, I leaned out the window and inhaled the cool, clean Maine air. "Taste that air," I said. "You can't get air like this at the Jersey Shore, and it's all mine for just eighty dollars and ninety cents a month."

The tremulous cry of a loon greeted us as we piled out of the bus. The lake sparkled in the setting sun. "Let's go for a swim,"

Sally said. It was a great idea. We were hot and tired from the ride. A swim in the cool, clear waters of Kezar would invigorate us. We quickly unpacked and changed into our suits. Wading into Kezar reminded me of that swim we'd taken at Jordan's late one night. It felt like we were slipping into silk.

As we splashed around, I noticed that we were getting appraising looks from a party at the cabin next door. My neighbors, a middle-aged couple whom I'd never met, were having a Fourth of July cookout. Two dozen or so very proper-looking people were sipping cocktails from very proper-looking plastic cups. They seemed to be taking a particular interest in Sally and Ruth. Their New York bikinis were definitely more suited to the Jersey Shore than Kezar Lake.

Every time Sally climbed up on the dock, she drew long stares, especially from the men. Sally was a tall, buxom beauty, and her suit, what there was of it, was bright silver. On Sally, the suit really shone. Kezar was a very conservative place. I was sure the folks next door hadn't seen anything like Sally and her suit since the days of Rudy Vallee.

Rudy Vallee was Kezar's most famous sport. During his heyday, Rudy used to import showgirls from New York and squire them around the lake in *Banjo Eyes,* a seventy-five-foot cabin cruiser given to him by his good friend Eddie Cantor. According to old-timers, the girls would sunbathe nude on the deck. Sally and Ruth must have reminded the men of Vallee girls. On Kezar, Rudy's adventures were legend.

"Let's go for a ride," I said to Clark. "I've got a three-horse-power Evinrude we can put on the canoe. We'll go up to Middle Bay and watch the sunset. It should be spectacular." Actually, I was going to show off. I wanted Clark and Sally to see some of the grand camps. Just being on the same lake as Severance Lodge had to be worth $80.90 a month.

We lugged the *Ruda* from under the porch and hitched on

the old Evinrude. I got in the stern, put Ruth and Sally in the middle, and told Clark to shove off.

"Just a minute," Clark said. He ran up to the bus and came back with a fishing rod. "Who knows," he said, "we might get lucky."

"But you don't have a license," I said. "That could be trouble. On a big weekend like this, the warden might be out."

"No problem," Clark said. "I'm an experienced fisherman. I can spot a warden a mile away."

What were the odds? There was only one warden in the whole Saco Valley, and he probably was home celebrating the Fourth of July. I gave the cord on the Evinrude a pull, and the motor sputtered into action. As we puttered past the neighbors, we waved politely. A couple of old codgers hoisted their drinks in honor of Sally's suit.

We were putting through the Narrows looking at loons when I noticed a dark green Ford parked on the bridge. A man in a dark green uniform was leaning on the rail looking at us through binoculars. I knew right away it was the warden. Clark, who claimed he could spot a warden a mile away, never saw him. He was too busy casting into the weeds trying to raise a bass. Dollar signs flashed through my head. The fine for fishing without a license was now up to seventy-five dollars, plus court costs. That equaled a month's payment to Norway Savings. As host, I was responsible, and I couldn't afford a fine.

The *Ruda* nearly capsized as we spun around. "Hey, what's going on?" Clark yelled.

"It's getting dark. We'd better get back," I shouted. I knew that sound travels clearly over water and I didn't want the warden to think we were running away. I pushed the throttle to full and made a beeline for the cabin. I remembered how Dad had outrun the warden on Lovewell. If we could make it to the cabin, we'd be safe.

Clark was confused. "Not enough light?" he yelled. "The sun's still up!" He still hadn't seen the warden.

"That man on the bridge is waving to us," Sally said.

"Good. Wave back," I told her. "People up here are very friendly."

I fiddled with the mixture, just like Dad had done, trying to coax more speed out of the Evinrude. There was a belch of blue smoke as the three little horses coughed and wheezed. They were getting old, and the four of us were too much for them. We were going nowhere, slowly.

"He's looking at us through binoculars," Ruth shouted. "I think it's the warden. Clark, you'd better hide that rod." Thanks, Ruth. Apparently, sound didn't carry over water on the Jersey Shore.

My back was to the bridge, but Sally was keeping me updated. "He just jumped into his car," she said.

Clark, the experienced fisherman, finally figured it out. He was shoving the rod onto the floor of the *Ruda*. "Let's get out of here," he yelled. "Open 'er up."

"She's open," I yelled back. I looked over my shoulder. The green Ford was gone. "Where is he? Can you see him?"

Clark pointed to a cloud of dust filtering up through the pines along the Ladies Delight road. "We can make it," he said.

We almost did. We were passing the lot next to our neighbors' when the warden came running out of the woods. He jumped onto a big rock on the shore and began waving us in. Seeing the warden, the bulk of the party hustled over to find out what was happening.

"There's the warden," squealed Sally. She tugged up the top of her bikini and waved. All the men waved back. I made believe I didn't see anybody and pushed the *Ruda* into a ninety-degree turn. We were heading to the other side of the Narrows.

"Sally," I said, leaning close to her. "Tell me what the warden's doing, but keep your voice down. Sound travels over water."

"He's still waving," she whispered. "I think he wants us to pull in."

Fat chance, I thought. "Let's go to the other side," I shouted, knowing the warden could hear me. "From there we can get a great view of the mountains."

"He stopped waving," Sally whispered. "He's running back toward his car." Beautiful, I thought. I had a plan.

"Sally," I whispered, "tell Ruth to tell Clark to keep an eye on the bridge."

Sally whispered to Ruth, who whispered to Clark, who whispered back to Ruth, who whispered to Sally, who whispered to me. "Ruth said that Clark said, 'Why?'"

"To look for the warden, you idiot!" I yelled. Then, regaining my composure, I leaned forward as far as I could and said to Clark, "If we can lure the warden back over the bridge and down the other side of the Narrows, we'll make a dash back to the cabin. By the time he gets turned around, you should be able to get the rod back in the bus."

Clark gave me a thumbs-up and began squinting at the bridge. We were almost to the opposite side of the Narrows when he pointed at a car crossing the bridge. The car was going fast and I thought it looked green, but it was getting dark and I couldn't be sure. It might have been the warden. "Head back," Clark yelled. "That's him."

"Are you sure?" I asked. Clark nodded. He could spot a warden a mile away, and the bridge was less than a half mile. I jerked the Evinrude around. "Sally," I said, leaning over, "when we reach the cabin, you and Ruth jump out and run up to the porch. Don't stop for anything." Sally nodded and turned to tell Ruth.

I took a deep breath of the cool, clean Maine air and looked up at the mountains silhouetted against the purple and orange sky. It was indeed a spectacular view. I just prayed I'd have $80.90 left to pay for it.

We hit the beach at full throttle. Clark jumped out with his rod, but that's as far as he got. "All right," a voice barked, "hold it right there." It was the warden. He'd been standing behind a tree by the side of the cabin. Sally and Ruth, true to the plan, completely ignored him. They nearly bounced out of their little suits as they bounded from the *Ruda.* There were audible gasps from the party next door, all with drinks in hand. Nobody had seen anything like this on Kezar since Rudy Vallee.

Clark, the experienced sportsman, had done just what the warden had told him. He was frozen on the beach, still holding his rod. "Ayuh," the warden said, eyeing the rod. "Let's see ya license."

I looked at his name tag. Damn! It was the infamous Ervin Lord, the same warden who'd nailed Viola Cunningham and the good Samaritan. Ignorance of the law was not going to get us off. I'd better come up with something original or our fragile budget would be busted. I looked up and saw Ruth and Sally on the porch in their New York suits. That gave me an idea. I'd try the Rudy Vallee defense.

"Ah, Officer Lord," I said, motioning the warden aside. "You see, we weren't really fishing." I paused and nodded toward the porch. "They're a couple of showgirls we brought up from New York. We wanted to let 'em think they'd been fishing in Maine. You know, show 'em a good time. Like Rudy Vallee used to."

The Warden looked at the *Ruda* and the little Evinrude. "Ain't exactly ol' *Banjo Eyes,*" he said suspiciously.

I pointed to our modest cabin and the '62 VW bus. "Well, we're not exactly Rudy Vallee, but we're giving it our best shot."

The warden thought about it for a second. He'd heard them all, but he seemed to like this one. He took the rod from Clark and studied the lure. "Ayuh, I guess I can believe that. No real fisherman would be using a Hula Dancer." Clark, the experienced fisherman, looked crushed, but he was in no position to defend himself. "How many life preservahs ya got?"

I counted the seat cushions that served as life preservers. "Ah, three," I said.

"Need foah. One for each passengah. State law, ya know." The warden pulled out his book and began writing a summons. "'Fraid that'll cost ya ten dollahs." Ten bucks! We could handle that. The Rudy Vallee defense had worked.

"Thanks a lot, Officer Lord," I said. "I really appreciate your help."

"No problem," he said, "but ya'd better get yaself another life preservah. And like Rudy Vallee used to say, if you're goin' fishin' with them showgirls, be careful ya don't catch nuthin.' Haw, haw."

ONE OVER
OUR LIMIT

My friend Ramsay fancies himself a real bass man. I met him at the University of Virginia business school. When Ramsay wasn't studying, he was fishing. Ramsay had married a local girl whose father had a bass pond right behind the house. He kept it filled with largemouth bass—big, lazy lunkers that just lay there waiting to be fed. He'd let Ramsay hook into a couple whenever he came out for a visit. Ramsay visited his in-laws a lot.

After business school, Ramsay had taken a prestigious position with the Boston Consulting Group. By chance, he moved to my old hometown of Arlington. I knew he was in trouble. There weren't any bass ponds around Arlington.

Ruth and I fled New York in the spring of 1970. Ruth had liked her job; I'd hated mine. Dealing with parking-lot owners in New York City was nothing like dealing with Mr. Severance. Plus, living in the city was no fun. There were theaters and lots of good restaurants and the best stores, but we couldn't afford them. What good was it being in the city if we were always on the outside looking in? When some Ivy Leaguers offered me a job syndicating recreational real estate in northern New England, I jumped at it.

When I called Ramsay to tell him we were back in town, all he wanted to talk about was fishing. He sounded desperate. He'd tried fishing all over the Northeast and was convinced that there wasn't a single bass north of the Mason-Dixon Line. Clark Smyth had told Ramsay about my cabin in Maine and had said he was sure I knew some good fishing spots. "Can you help me?" Ramsay pleaded.

"Don't worry," I told him. "I know a pond in Lovell that's loaded with smallmouth bass. In fact, I'm going up to the cabin this weekend. Why don't you come with me and we'll do some fishing."

Ramsay was parked outside my door the first thing Saturday morning. His canoe was tied to the top of his station wagon. The back of the wagon was loaded with rods, reels, and tackle boxes. Ramsay's objective was clearly defined by two decals on the side window. One read "Stop Wishin' and Start Fishin'"; the other read "B.A.S.S.," the official insignia of the Bass Anglers Sportsmen's Society.

Ramsay made me read aloud from *McClane's Standard Fishing Encyclopedia* as we made our way north. The chapter on bass was dog-eared and thoroughly annotated. The part he liked best was the section called "Angling Value." It stated: "The smallmouth bass is widely acclaimed as the top trophy of the bass family. The fish is extremely active and usually jumps when hooked. The average smallmouth is not nearly as large as many freshwater fish, but the capture of a four- to five-pounder requires more skill and more patience than the taking of many species of comparable size." Ramsay had me read that part several times.

In Fryeburg, we stopped at Solari's and bought our licenses.

Clark had warned Ramsay to be sure to get a license. When we crossed the bridge at the Narrows, I told Ramsay, "Turn left at the next road. We'll go to the cabin and unload our stuff."

Ramsay kept going. "Let's scout out the pond first," he said. "We can unload later." Ramsay was like a horse heading to the barn. I thought he was going to wreck his car as we bounced over the rocks and around the gullies on the road to Horseshoe Pond. Ramsay hardly slowed down. It was time to "Stop Wishin' and Start Fishin'."

After we parked, I wanted to walk up the logging road and look at my lots. Ramsay insisted we launch the canoe immediately. He wanted to scout the pond for submerged rocks and logs and other spots where bass might be hiding. I paddled while Ramsay peered at the bottom and tested the water temperature with his official B.A.S.S. thermometer. Except for one new cabin on one of the lots by the town landing, nothing had changed on Horseshoe since I'd bought my lots. The pond was still natural and wild, a developer's dream, and now that I was a developer, I started dreaming. Horseshoe Pond was a lot nicer than any of the places the Ivy Leaguers were syndicating. Maybe I should bring it to their attention.

Once we'd circled the entire pond, Ramsay consulted his solunar tables and proclaimed that 7:25 P.M. would be the optimum time to start fishing. "Let's take the canoe back and recheck some of those sites," he said.

"You go ahead," I told him. "I'm going to walk around for a while."

While Ramsay paddled, I walked the shoreline marking off potential lots. Back at the cabin, while Ramsay fiddled with his equipment, I sketched out plot plans. I was playing with some pro formas when Ramsay announced it was time to start fishing. At precisely 7:25 P.M. we hit the water.

Now Ramsay took total command. He put me in the bow and

told me we'd paddle about thirty yards from shore, trolling a line on each side of the canoe. I tied on a Rapala, an underwater lure that looks like a minnow. Ramsay scoffed at my Rapala. "Overrated," he said. He chose a Tony Accetta Jelly Belly with the Glow Eyes. "When they see these Glow Eyes, they'll be jumping into the canoe."

It felt good to be fishing again, especially on a deserted pond with no motors. The last time Dad and I fished Lovewell, we cruised the whole lake with the Evinrude and ended up with three little perch. Bigger boats and bigger camps had sprouted up all over Lovewell. We never saw schools of fish anymore, Old Tom was long gone, and despite the motors and new equipment, fishing wasn't as much fun. Lovewell had been fished out.

I was lost in the past when I felt a strong jerk on my line. I looked back and saw a smallmouth leap out of the water. Ramsay was ecstatic; it was the first smallmouth he'd ever seen. The fish lived up to McClane's billing. The capture did indeed "require more skill and more patience that the taking of many species of comparable size." Ramsay skillfully netted the bass and proceeded to study it in great detail. He weighed and measured the fish, then carefully photographed it from several angles before releasing it. He was sure that in a matter of minutes he would be posing with one of his own.

It didn't happen. My Rapala hooked another beauty, which Ramsay didn't bother to photograph. He was too busy changing lures. His second selection was Bagley's Famous Mud Bug. He lovingly tied it to the end of his line and beamed as he watched it wriggle through the water. "My father-in-law's bass stand in line to get a shot at this baby," he told me.

By nine o'clock, the Rapala had scored again, but the Mud Bug had lured only one fish, and it had thrown the hook. The real bugs were getting bad, and I was ready to quit. I wanted to get back to the cabin, start a fire, and grill up some steaks, but

Ramsay insisted we make one last run. Since the water was calm, he'd decided to switch to a surface lure. I watched as he rummaged through his tackle box weighing the pros and cons of several layers of lures. He finally settled upon Fred Arbogast's classic Double-Lobed Lip Jitterbug. This particular model had the markings of a green frog and two sets of treble hooks.

It was totally dark by the time we started back to the landing. We were each trailing about twenty-five yards of line when Ramsay announced he had a strike. We couldn't see the Jitterbug, but we heard two splashes and assumed they were the customary jumps of a smallmouth bass. I reeled in my line and grabbed the net.

Ramsay was positive he had a big one. "Let's hear it for Fred Arbogast! This could be a new school and pool!" he shouted. "This mother's really jumping!" Then there was a dramatic change in his voice. "Hey," he said anxiously, "something's wrong here." He was holding the rod vertically over his head, reeling frantically.

"Ramsay, get your rod down. You're going to lose him if he comes up."

"Comes up? He's already up. He's someplace over my head!"

"What?"

At that moment, a large white object came soaring over the canoe and slammed into the water. McClane would have been very proud. Ramsay was still playing it for all he was worth. "Get the light!" he screamed. "Get the light!"

"What light?"

"The one in my tackle box."

I leaned back, but I couldn't reach his tackle box. By this time, Ramsay's "fish" had taken off again. It circled the canoe and crashed into the woods.

"Ramsay," I said, "you must have caught a bird. Hold the line, and I'll paddle us to shore."

"The hell with that," he said. "I'm cutting this line before whatever it is comes back."

I started to protest, but Ramsay cut the line before I could say anything. We could hear the bird in the woods, trying to shake the Jitterbug. "Let's get back to camp," Ramsay said. He was not pleased.

Memories of Old Tom fishing on Lovewell came back to me. Could Ramsay possibly have hooked an eagle? "Wait a minute," I said, "we can't leave that bird. It might be an eagle."

"Whatever it is, it's big, and it's mean," Ramsay replied. "Besides, what chance do we have of finding it in the dark?"

We heard the tinkle of hooks as the bird continued to try to free itself. A light had come on at the one lone cabin at the far end of Horseshoe. "I'll tell you what," I said. "Let's go down to that cabin. Maybe there are some kids there who can help us."

We paddled down and introduced ourselves to Dick and Pat de La Chapelle and their four children. The de La Chapelles couldn't believe that Ramsay had hooked a bird. The kids quickly ran off to find it. We stumbled along the shore behind them. After half an hour, we'd found nothing. We were just about to give up when we heard the hooks tinkling under a bush. I turned the light towards the sound and saw two huge brown eyes glaring at me. The bird wasn't an eagle; it was a barred owl, and its beak and talons were hooked together by Fred Arbogast's classic Double-Lobed Lip Jitterbug.

Ramsay's line was hanging from the branch of a tree. The owl must have tried to gain a perch and fallen into the bush. One of the kids started toward the bird. Dick de La Chapelle pulled him back. "Watch it," he said. "If that bird gets excited, you could lose an eye."

He was right; the combination of beak, talons, and hooks made the owl very dangerous. "Let's see if we can get it back to the cabin, where we can take a good look at it," I said. I took off my jacket, one of those heavy, red-and-black wool shirts made by Woolrich, and threw it over the owl.

Back at the cabin, I placed the bird on the picnic table, next to Dick de La Chapelle's big kerosene lantern. I gingerly removed my jacket. The bird lay there, studying me with its huge brown eyes. Now that I had more light, I could see that two hooks were embedded in its right talon. That must have happened when it hit the lure. Then, in its efforts to free itself, it had put a hook into its left talon and another into its beak.

"Ramsay," I said. "Get in here and help me clean your fish."

Ramsay was standing back with the de La Chapelles. Dick was still trying to restrain his curious kids. "You've got to be kidding," Ramsay said.

"Come on, it's just a bird."

"It's not just a bird; it's a big bird, with a big beak, big talons, and big hooks."

I knew that Ramsay was right, but I had to try to free this bird, and to do that I needed his help. "Come on. All you have to do is hold the wings and consult. I'll do the cutting."

The idea of consulting must have appealed to Ramsay. He stepped forward and grabbed the owl by both wings. I took a pair of pliers and went to work. I had no idea what the owl might do when I freed its beak and talons. "Ramsay," I said, "if it starts to attack me, let it go."

"Don't worry," Ramsay said. "If that bird moves, I'm out of here." I could see the sweat on Ramsay's brow and felt a bead trickling down my own nose.

First I freed the beak, then the left talon. The bird was still watching me with its huge brown eyes, but it didn't move. I sensed it knew that I was trying to help. I sure hoped that was the case because the right talon presented the real problem. The barbs on the hooks were in so deep that I couldn't pull them out. The only way to remove them was to push them all the way through. That was going to hurt. "Hang on," I said to Ramsay, and gave the hooks a push. Remarkably, the bird just lay there. It must have been in shock.

"Okay, Ramsay, nice going," I said, removing the last of the hooks. "Your consulting job is over."

Ramsay looked very relieved as he moved back to where the de La Chapelles were standing. As I wrapped the owl back into my jacket, I felt like John J. Audubon, Aldo Leopold, and Noah all rolled into one. I picked up the bird and brought it down to the de La Chapelle's dock. Lying on the dock swaddled in my Woolrich with only its head showing, the owl looked like a baby with extra big eyes and a funny haircut. "Ramsay, quick, take a picture," I said. "You can send it to your father-in-law. Show him what you catch in Maine." Ramsay got one shot of his owl before it wriggled free, defecated on my jacket, and flew off into the night.

We fished again the next morning. As we paddled around the Frog, I was thinking how Horseshoe had the potential for a low-density development, one that would retain the wild feeling of the pond. All Ramsay was thinking about was fish. He'd switched to his ultimate weapon, the Sidewinder, made by the Acme Tackle Company. My Rapala caught one more nice bass, but the Sidewinder came up empty. Ramsay had yet to catch a fish.

I was in high spirits as we drove back to Boston. I couldn't wait to tell Ruth about our adventure with the owl, and fishing Horseshoe Pond had given me the same wilderness feeling I used to get at Jordan's. I suggested to Ramsay that we come back the following weekend. He was noncommittal. He seemed to have lost interest in discussing the angling value of small-mouth bass.

I called Ramsay at his office a few days later to see if he

wanted to go back to Horseshoe. His secretary told me that he was out of town on personal business and wouldn't be back until the following week. When I asked where Ramsay had gone, she said, "Virginia. He needed to visit his father-in-law."

THE RENTERS FROM HAVERHILL

The only way Ruth and I could afford to keep the cabin on Kezar was by renting it out. I was having a tough time trying to establish myself as a developer. Getting to know the market and the players in it was taking a long time, and I didn't like working for the Ivy Leaguers. When I'd joined them, they'd billed themselves as "conservation developers." After a year, I was still looking for the conservation. All I'd seen from the Ivy Leaguers were cookie-cutter developments. Meanwhile, having to write a check every month to Norway Savings for $80.90, plus $107 a year in taxes to the town of Lovell, plus another $100 for insurance, was a burden that hung over Ruth and me like a dark cloud.

As part of my ongoing education in real estate, I'd discovered that a summer cabin in Maine was not a good investment for OPM. OP demanded their M back every month, and a summer cabin in Maine only produced income for ten weeks. Bugs killed the spring and cold, the fall, at least for renters. If the cabin was going to pay for itself, we had to make hay while the sun shined. We had to rent it every week from the Fourth of July through Labor Day.

On the Friday before Memorial Day, I placed the following ad in the *Boston Globe*: "FOR RENT: Cabin on btfl Kezar Lake, Lovell, Me., $125/wk with canoe. 617-925-4672 aft 5."

That evening the phone rang. "You the one renting the cabin in Maine?" the voice asked.

"Yes, I am. What can I tell you about it?"

"How many bedrooms?"

"Three, but they're small. How many are you?"

"Me an' my wife an' three kids, but they're little."

"That would be okay."

"What's the town like?"

"There's not much to Lovell, but the cabin is on Kezar, the most beautiful lake in Maine. Are you familiar with Kezar Lake?"

"Ya got a TV?"

A TV? "No, there's no TV." The guy sounded a little rough. I began to wonder if he was our type of renter. "May I ask where you're calling from?"

"Haverhill," the guy said. "I want to get the wife and kids out of the city for a while."

Haverhill? That raised an immediate red flag. People from Haverhill didn't go to Kezar, even the Lower Bay. I had a plan for screening out people who I didn't think would be desirable. I'd ask them what weeks they wanted to rent and tell them the cabin was already booked. "When would you be wanting to go?" I said.

"Tomorrow."

Tomorrow? Who'd want to go to Maine in May? This guy must be some doofus looking for a place to spend Memorial Day weekend. "I'm sorry," I said. "We don't rent weekends. It's too much trouble."

"I want it for the month," the guy said.

A month? Well, that was a different story. I never thought we'd see a nickel from the cabin in June. Renting it for the whole month would do wonders for our cash flow. Still, I had an uneasy feeling about this guy from Haverhill. "You going to be home tonight?" I asked.

"I guess so, why?" he said.

"My wife and I are going to Andover to look at a car. We could drop by and meet you. There's another guy who wants the cabin for June, but maybe I can move him around."

"Okay," he said, and gave me the directions.

Ruth had taken a job at Wellesley College and needed a car. I'd found what seemed like a good one in Andover for $500. Andover was next to Haverhill, so I figured we could stop and check out this potential renter, then go look at the car.

Haverhill was a mill town with no operating mills. The textile industry had long ago taken its business south to the land of no unions, cheap labor, and King Cotton. All that Haverhill produced these days was urban decay, and it was doing a good job of that. I shuddered as our '67 VW Bug pulled up in front of the address the guy had given me. It was a three-story tenement. Our potential renter lived on the top floor. Ruth gave me a dubious look as we climbed the old wooden stairs. By the time we reached the top, I'd made my decision. I was going to tell this guy I'd talked with the other renter who wanted it for June and he'd said his vacation was fixed. There was no way he could change it. Sorry.

I knocked on the door. A weaselly little guy with mossy teeth opened it. Ruth's stepfather is a dentist, so her first impression of people starts with their teeth. This guy was off to a bad start. "Come in," he said, looking furtively up and down the hall. "The place is kind of a mess."

Cheap plastic toys were scattered all over the floor, clothes were thrown on the chairs, a TV blared in the background.

Three pretty little girls were sitting around a table eating maca-roni and cheese. They all needed their faces washed. The wife, a cute blond, was standing by the sink making a feeble effort to wash a stack of dirty dishes. She was as white as a sheet and had dark bags under her eyes. She looked totally wiped out. I couldn't wait to get out of this place. "Look," I said to the guy, "I talked with the fellow who wants the cabin for June, and he said he'd already put in for his vacation time and it was too late to change, so . . ."

The guy motioned me aside. "My wife just had a miscarriage," he whispered. "I was hoping I could get her away. I'd appreciate anything you could do to help."

The kids were staring at Ruth, their eyes big as saucers. The smallest one got up from the table and came over and took Ruth's hand. "Want to see my doll?" she said.

"Sarah, leave the lady alone," her mother said. It was obvi-ous that the miscarriage had beaten the hell out of her.

"That's okay. I'd love to see her doll," Ruth said.

"We're going to Maine," one of the other girls said, jumping up and taking Ruth's other hand. These kids were really cute.

"That's exciting," Ruth said. "You'll like Maine. It's very pretty. You can swim, and go for rides in the canoe, and listen to the loons."

This was not going as planned. "Ahhh, Ruth," I said, "could I see you for a moment?" I turned to the guy. "Could you excuse us, please?" Ruth and I stepped outside.

"What the hell are you doing?" I said. "We don't want these people in our cabin."

"Why not?" she said. "They seem very nice, and they need a vacation. Look at that poor woman and those little kids. Who are we to make judgments?"

I thought about the $600. Ruth was right. Who were we to make judgments. "Okay," I said, "but let me handle the negotiations."

We went back in. "We know another camp where we can send this other fellow, so if you want the cabin for all of June, it's yours."

"Good," the guy said. "How much?"

"Well, the whole month is a little more than four weeks, so that'd be six hundred dollars." I looked at the wife and kids. "But the weather can be iffy in June, so make it five." Ruth smiled. We were doing the right thing.

"Okay," the guy said. He went over to the cupboard, took out a coffee can, and emptied it on the table. A big wad of bills rolled out. He counted out five hundred in fives, tens, and twenties, and handed them to me. "Here you go, five hundred."

I couldn't believe it. "Gee, that's a lot of money to keep lying around," I said.

"I'm a painter," the guy said. "I just collected on a big job."

We gave them directions to the camp, told them where to find the key, and wished them luck. An hour later, I handed the five hundred to the former owner of Ruth's new car. All in all, it had been a very successful day.

Toward the end of June, I was feeling pretty good about my life. I'd quit syndicating recreational real estate with the Ivy Leaguers and was trading stocks for a fellow I knew who had a seat on the Boston Stock Exchange. It wasn't steady work, but along with Ruth's job at Wellesley, it was enough to keep us going. I'd sent my resume to several national conservation organizations and had gotten a feeler back from The Nature Conservancy. From what I'd been able to find out, The Nature Conservancy was a little group headquartered in Washington, D.C., that bought land for conservation. Davis Cherington, the director of stewardship, was coming to Boston in August and wanted to meet with me. Davis told me that he too had worked for the Ivy Leaguers and was "damn glad to get out." I took that as a positive sign.

On the last Wednesday in June, I was in our apartment watching *F Troop,* my favorite TV show, when the phone rang. "Is this the David Morine who owns a cabin on Kezar Lake?" the voice said.

"Yes, it is."

"This is Sheriff Andrews callin' from Fryeburg. Ya got some people stayin' at your place?"

"Yes, I've rented it to a family from Haverhill."

"Ya know these people?"

"No, sir." This didn't sound good.

"So ya don't know 'em, and they're just rentin'?"

"That's right, Sheriff. Is there some problem?"

"Had any contact with 'em, say in the last few days?"

"No, sir. May I ask what this is about?"

"How long they stayin'?" Sheriff Andrews wasn't giving any answers and was making me more nervous with each question.

"They've rented it for all of June. Are they all right?"

"Ya sure ya don't know 'em and had no contact with 'em?"

"Positive. Look, Sheriff, my family's been going to Maine for a long time. There are plenty of people up there who know us. What's this all about?"

"Ayuh, I've checked ya out. Didn't think you were part of it."

"Part of what?"

"We think ya rentas are plannin' to rob the Lovell Post Office."

"What!"

"Ayuh, FBI got a tip. I've staked 'em out, but looks like they've taken off. Thought ya might've heard from 'em."

"I can give you a phone number in Haverhill."

"No need. FBI's got it." Then the sheriff added, "Ya got a TV there?"

"No. Why?"

"Ya neighbor reported one missin'. Them renters been watchin' it every night. Seen the glow."

I felt a knot growing in my stomach. "Is there anything I can do?" I said. I was hoping the sheriff would tell me not to worry, that these things happen every now and then, and that he'd take care of it. No such luck.

"You'd best get up here," he said. "I want to get in there and look around. You could tell me what's yours and what they stole."

"When?"

"How 'bout tomorrow?"

"What if they haven't left? What if they're still there?"

"I can handle 'em," the sheriff said.

Gawd, I hoped they were gone. I didn't want to watch this guy get arrested. What about his cute wife and three little girls— who was going to take care of them? I wanted nothing to do with this situation, but I agreed to meet the sheriff at Solari's in Fryeburg at noon the next day.

Crossing the line would have none of the pleasure I usually felt when entering Maine. "Vacationland" had become "Problemland." I remembered Dad telling Mom when she was badgering him to buy a place, "Donna, I didn't come to Maine to work and worry. I came here to relax." Now I knew what he was talking about.

Sheriff Richard Andrews was sitting in his squad car waiting for me. When I pulled the VW Bug into a space in front of Solari's, he motioned for me to get into the squad car with him. Even sitting down, Sheriff Andrews was a big man. The neatly trimmed hair below the rim of his Smokey the Bear hat suggested a military background. The powerful arms bulging from his short-sleeve shirt showed he was in good shape. The worn look of the revolver resting on his hip indicated it had been fired often. If I were a weasely little crook from Haverhill, I wouldn't want to mess with Sheriff Richard Andrews.

"Sheriff Andrews, Dave Morine," I said, extending my hand. The sheriff shook it with a firm grip.

"Ayuh. Appreciate ya comin'."

"Well, I'm sorry about this trouble. What do you want me to do?"

"Figure we'll ride up there and look around. Staked out ya place last night. No sign of 'em, but it'd be best to leave your car here and ride with me. Don't want to do nothin' to tip 'em off. This guy's armed and dangerous."

"You still think he's going to rob the post office?"

"Can't tell, but it's sure got Sam Ring jumpy." Sam Ring was the postmaster in Lovell.

"Sheriff," I said as we headed north on Route 5, "I've been wondering. Why would anybody want to rob a post office? What are they going to steal, stamps?"

"Stamps, ha, that's a good one." The sheriff chuckled. "Rural post offices are loaded with money."

"What?"

"No banks. Businesspeople can't afford to be runnin' to Norway or Fryeburg every day to make a deposit. That's an hour round-trip, so instead they go to the post office, buy a money order, and mail it in. Town like Lovell's got the marina, the market, the Center Lovell Store, all buyin' money orders. By the end of the day, post office's got plenty of cash."

"I never thought of that," I said, "but then, I'm not a crook."

"Here, ya might want to look at this," the sheriff said, reaching under the seat and handing me a file. "FBI" was printed in big black letters on the cover. A tab in the corner had the name of my renter typed on it.

I opened the file. There were two police photos of my renter stapled to the inside, one head-on, the other in profile, both showing the same lousy teeth. Opposite the photos was a stack of arrest reports. I started thumbing through them. This guy was no small-time crook. He'd been arrested for armed robbery, possession of illegal firearms, vehicular theft, even one murder. Apparently, he was pretty good at it. There were no major convictions.

I was particularly interested in the last report. My renter was suspected of robbing a drugstore in Haverhill the very day that Ruth and I had met him. "Wow," I said to the sheriff, "they think this guy robbed a drugstore the same day we met him."

"Paid ya in cash, right?" the sheriff said.

"Yes, five hundred dollars. How'd you know?"

"'Cause he got it at the drugstore, that's how."

"Really?" I said. "This guy must have brass balls. He walks into a drugstore right in Haverhill, robs them, then gives me the cash to pay for his vacation. How'd the FBI find out he planned to rob the post office?"

"Wife's brother's doin' time in a federal penitentiary. Your renter wrote him and told him how easy it'd be to rob the post office. Said he thought he'd give it a try. Brother-in-law called the feds to make a deal. Robbin' a post office is a federal offense."

"Nice family," I said.

We eased into Lovell. I couldn't look at the post office. Poor Sam Ring, and it was all my fault. As we pulled onto the road to Ladies Delight, the sheriff stopped. He took out his revolver and spun the cylinder around to make sure it was fully loaded. "When we get there," he said, "you stay in the car. I'll go down an' check the cabin."

"Yes, sir," I said. I wasn't going near that cabin.

There was no car when we got there. The sheriff pulled up, got out, and walked down to the cabin. I'd given him a key, but the door was open. If you're the crook, I guess you don't worry about getting robbed. After a few minutes, the sheriff signaled me to come join him.

The cabin was a total mess. Dirty dishes were piled high in the sink. Dirty diapers were on the floor. Kids' clothes were lying all around, but the neighbors' TV was gone. "Left in a hurry," the sheriff said, opening the refrigerator. It was full of food and needed to be defrosted. The place smelled like a kennel.

"Gawd, it stinks in here," I said.

"Must have been that puppy. Doubt it was trained," the sheriff said. I guess they'd gotten the girls a pet.

Sheriff Andrews went through the trash and found some letters from the brother in the federal penitentiary. The brother thought some guy was messing around with his girl and wanted my renters to kill him. These were bad people, like Bonnie and Clyde. "You sure picked some good ones," the sheriff scoffed. "Too bad we missed 'em."

I got the distinct impression that Sheriff Andrews was disappointed. I was very glad to have missed them. Ruth and I had let them into our special place and they'd destroyed it. We'd never be able to go back to the cabin without worrying that they might show up. These weren't the renters from Haverhill; they were the renters from hell.

I METAMORPHOSIS

The outer half of the Frog on Horseshoe Pond was owned by the Stone sisters, four proper ladies who had inherited a lot of land in Lovell. In addition to the Frog, the Stone sisters owned the entire northwest corner of Kezar Lake. This huge holding on the Upper Bay included a spectacular peninsula known as Rattlesnake Island, which was where the Stones, a prominent Boston family, had built their summer compound. The three rustic camps and modest boathouse dated back to the era when Kezar had been a prime destination for big-time sports. Motoring around Rattlesnake Island had been one of the highlights of Mom's annual tour of Kezar. She liked the simple lines of the boathouse and cottages. Plus, the Stones' beach was the nicest on Kezar, all natural sand and very private.

I met the Stone sisters through an old high school friend, Bobby Harrington. Ruth and I were surprised to bump into Bobby and his wife, Cheryl, at the Center Lovell Store. I hadn't seen Bobby in ten years. He was an avid fisherman and told us that in his search for the perfect lake, he'd discovered Kezar. We were really surprised when we asked Bobby and Cheryl where they were staying, and they said at the Stones'.

"You're on Rattlesnake Island?" I asked, surprised. Bobby was a kid from Arlington. Like me, he had no business being on the Upper Bay.

"Nooo, we're not on the island," Bobby said, recognizing my surprise. "The Stone sisters have a couple of camps on the road coming in. To help pay the taxes, they rent them out. A fishing buddy of mine knows them and got us in. Why don't you and Ruth come up for a swim?"

As renters, Bobby and Cheryl had beach privileges. I remembered puttering past the beach in our little boat from the marina and thinking, "Boy, I'd sure like to go swimming there." I immediately accepted Bobby's invitation.

It was on the beach that I meet the Stone sisters. They were very cordial and interested that I owned land next to theirs on the Frog. They told me their father had been an avid fisherman and had bought the land on the Frog so he could build a fish camp on the tip. That's where he went when he really wanted to get away. I said I could see why and mentioned that if they ever decided to sell the Frog, I hoped they'd let me know.

That was late August 1971. I was still trading stocks on the Boston Stock Exchange, but I'd met with Davis Cherington from The Nature Conservancy and we'd hit it off. I liked what he said about conservation and the Conservancy, and he liked my background in real estate and the fact that I'd been disillusioned with the Ivy Leaguers. Davis told me there'd be a position opening up at the national office at the end of the year and invited me to Washington to meet with more of the staff in early November. I got the feeling I'd be able to land a job with the Conservancy, but I wasn't sure I wanted to move to Washington.

In October the phone rang. We were living in an apartment

in Woburn, at the intersection of Routes 128 and 495, less than a mile from the cancer-causing wells that subsequently were exposed in the book and movie *A Civil Action.* Ruth answered the phone. "It's Sybil Stone," she said, cupping her hand over the receiver. "She wants to talk to you."

I took the phone from Ruth. "Hello, Miss Stone," I said, wondering why in the world one of the Stone sisters would be calling me. "What may I do for you?"

"Well, Mr. Morine, you mentioned when we met this summer that if we ever decided to sell the Frog, we should let you know. Mr. Hastings, our lawyer in Fryeburg, has just presented us with an offer that we're prepared to accept, but because you own the land next to us, we wanted to give you a chance to make a bid."

I nearly dropped the phone. When I was a developer, this call would have been my dream. Now that I was hoping to become a conservationist, it was a nightmare. Whoever was making this offer probably was going to develop the property. I knew from the pro formas I'd run when I was fishing with Ramsay that the most profitable plan would be to whack a road down the middle of the Frog and divide it into forty hundred-foot lots. That kind of development would make a lot of money but totally destroy the pond. That's why I'd never told the Ivy Leaguers about Horseshoe.

"Gee, Miss Stone, that's very kind of you," I said, my mind spinning, trying to come up with some type of plan. "Is there any chance I could come over and meet with you? Maybe we could reach some type of agreement."

There was silence on the other end of line. Apparently, Miss Stone hadn't expected me to suggest a meeting. If I wanted the land, I should just make an offer. "Could you hold, Mr. Morine? I'll have to confer with my sisters."

"Please do."

She was back in a moment. "Yes, we'd be happy to meet with you. Mr. Hastings wants an answer by tomorrow, so you should probably come tonight."

"Yes, I guess I should," I said, my hands shaking. "How would eight o'clock be?"

"That would be fine." Miss Stone proceeded to give me directions to their house in Belmont, which was two towns away. It was six o'clock. How was I ever going to come up with a plan in two hours?

"What did Miss Stone want?" Ruth asked.

"They're going to sell the Frog. They have an offer that they're prepared to accept, but based on our conversation this summer, they want to give me a chance to make a counteroffer."

"That's very nice of them," Ruth said. Ruth was always very upbeat and never seemed to worry about money. "I'm sure you can do it. How much time do you have?"

"Two hours," I said. "I'm screwed."

I pulled up to the Stones' promptly at eight. I still had no plan. I'd put a call into the de La Chapelles, but they weren't home. I'd left a message with one of the kids asking Dick or Pat to call me as soon as possible, but I knew the de La Chapelles were a shot in the dark. The only time I'd met them was when Ramsay caught his owl, and even though they'd impressed me as wonderful people, I also knew that they were staring at four college tuitions. I seriously doubted that the de la Chapelles were in a position to throw more money into land on Horseshoe Pond.

Only one of the Stone sisters was married. She lived in Rhode Island. The other three lived together in the family home in Belmont. Those were the three who were waiting to see me. After we sat down, Ruth, the oldest, explained to me that each of the sisters had a separate function regarding the management of their property in Maine. She was in charge of maintenance,

Ellen handled the rents, Alice paid the bills, and Sybil was in charge of the real estate. "So it's Sybil you'll be dealing with this evening," Ruth said.

I turned to Sybil. "Well, Miss Stone," I began, still not sure what I was going to say, "first and foremost, I appreciate you and your sisters being kind enough to give me this opportunity to meet with you regarding the Frog. My objective in making this purchase would be to protect as much of the land as possible. I think that Horseshoe Pond is a unique natural area that should be preserved. I'm just not sure how to do it. Is there any chance you could tell me about the offer you've received? If the person wants it all for himself or to build a family place like you have on Rattlesnake Island, there's no sense in my bidding against him."

Sybil hesitated, not sure how much she should tell me about the existing offer. She looked to her sisters for guidance. They nodded, indicating that she could proceed. "We don't want to get into a bidding contest, Mr. Morine," she said. "As I told you on the phone, we are prepared to accept the offer Mr. Hastings has presented to us. As for the intent of the buyer, we're not sure what he's planning to do with the property."

"May I ask what he's offering?" I said.

Once again, Sybil looked to her sisters for guidance. Once again, they nodded. "Sixty-five thousand dollars," Sybil said.

I did some quick calculations. Forty lots at $4,000 apiece would be $160,000, less 10 percent selling costs, another 10 per-cent for a survey and a road, plus legal fees and carrying costs. This guy was looking to double his money, which fit the formula for this type of development. The problem was trying to sell forty lots. Bill Severance had unloaded all sixty lots on Ladies Delight in one summer, but that was Kezar. This was Horseshoe, and Horseshoe had no power. One scenario I'd played with in preparing my pro formas was dividing the Frog into just ten lots, each with 400 feet of frontage. Ten more camps would not destroy the pond's natural uniqueness. The question was, if I offered the Stone sisters $70,000, could I find ten buyers at $10,000 each? After expenses, that would be my breakeven.

I took a deep breath. "Miss Stone," I said, "I would like to offer you seventy thousand with the restriction that the land could not be subdivided into more than ten single-family lots. I'd try to do less, but I think the land could hold up to ten camps without destroying the natural uniqueness of the pond."

The sisters looked at each other and nodded. I didn't know if it was the $70,000 or the ten-lot restriction that had caught their interest, but Sybil said, "That will be acceptable, Mr. Morine. How much are you willing to put down as a deposit?"

I began to shake. They'd actually accepted my offer and wanted a deposit. What was I going to do? I didn't have any money. I heard a voice talking, but I didn't recognize it as mine. "Would five hundred be acceptable?"

"That would be fine," Sybil said. "You realize, of course, we'll have to give the other bidder one chance to make a counter-offer, but we're not going to go back and forth. That will be it. If he bids more than you, it's his. If he passes, it's yours. We'd expect ten percent on the signing of the purchase and sale agreement and the balance at closing."

"Yes, of course," I said. At that point, I was in such shock that I would have agreed to anything. While Sybil wrote up the offer, I wrote the check. To this day I don't know where I found the courage to sign it.

I was still shaking when I walked into our apartment. "Ruth, how much money do we have in the checking account?" I asked.

"About three hundred dollars. Why?"

"Well, we're broke. I just signed a check for five hundred." I collapsed in a chair. "I made an offer to buy the Frog for seventy thousand. If they accept it and we can't come up with the money, we'll lose the five hundred."

"Don't worry," Ruth said. "Dick de La Chapelle called. When I told him you'd gone to meet with the Stone sisters about buying the Frog, he said to call him back, no matter how late. He was very interested."

I called Dick and told him what I'd done. He, like Ruth, said not to worry. He'd talked to Will Dagget, a heart surgeon and avid fisherman who'd recently bought the land next to the de La Chapelles on Horseshoe. "We're prepared to back you up," Dick said. "And the idea of restricting the land to no more than ten lots is excellent. If we have to, I'm sure we can find ten buyers at ten thousand apiece."

Talking with Dick made me feel better, but I still didn't sleep that night. It was my name on the offer and my five hundred dollars at risk. If the Stone sisters accepted my offer, I was going to have to scramble to find the money.

The next day, Sybil Stone called. She said that the other buyer had upped his offer to $75,000 and they had agreed to sell the land to him. I felt both relieved and disappointed. I was off the hook, but I'd lost Horseshoe Pond. If this guy whacked the Frog into forty lots, the pond would be gone. "But," Sybil added, "my sisters and I liked your restriction so much that we made it part of our contract. Under the terms of our sale, the Frog cannot be subdivided into more than ten single-family lots."

I couldn't believe it. The buyer, who was in fact a developer, eventually got the Stone sisters to increase the restriction to twelve lots, but still, my offer had kept Horseshoe Pond from becoming completely destroyed. Forget about negotiating parking-lot leases and syndicating recreational real estate, I wanted to save land. "If The Nature Conservancy offers me a job in Washington," I told Ruth, "we're going." My metamorphosis was complete. I was a conservationist.

BREAKING EVEN

Rocks talk to Rodney Jordan, really they do. They want to get his attention; they want him to make them a star. And Rodney can do it. He can pick up an ordinary rock sitting by the side of the road, dust it off, size it up, and cast it as part of one of his flawless fieldstone fireplaces. Once a rock catches Rodney's eye, it's set for life.

I first became aware of Rodney's talent when Ramsay caught his owl and we met the de La Chapelles. The de La Chapelle's cabin on Horseshoe Pond wasn't anything special, just one of those precut kits, but their fireplace was spectacular. It was big and solid, and every rock seemed to fit perfectly. I had to get up close to see the mortar. That was unusual. I'd always found fieldstones, particularly Maine fieldstones, to be ruggedly independent. They seemed to take pride in their steadfast resistance to any semblance of conformity. These stones looked like they'd been raised together. Whoever had built the de La Chapelle's fireplace had a rare touch.

When I asked Pat and Dick who'd done the work for them, they told me about Rodney Jordan. "Rodney's a real character," Pat said. "He lives up in Bethel, but he and his wife camped out here for two weeks while they built the fireplace. They got the rocks from old walls they found in the woods. Rodney used to work in the woods and knows all about nature." I decided right then and there that if I ever built a cabin on my lots, I'd find Rodney Jordan and ask him to make me a fieldstone fireplace.

On December 8, 1975, Mom passed away. Cancer. For the last twelve years of her life, Mom's main occupation was drafting and redrafting the plans for her cabin on Kezar. The whole time we were at Jordan's, she'd be driving around western Maine looking at homes, collecting ideas, trying to find a builder who shared her exacting standards of line and style. Mom's happiest moments were sitting on her favorite rock at Kezar, soaking up her view of the White Mountains and studying her plans.

In 1979, Dad sent me the deed to Mom's lot on Ladies Delight along with a trunk full of her plans. By then Dad had built a place in West Bath right across the New Meadows River from Ted's in-laws. Both Dad and Ted were sold on the coast and neither of them had any interest in Kezar. Bill was living in New Jersey and had no interest in Maine. Dad told me I could do whatever I wanted with Mom's lot. He was tired of paying the taxes. I told him I'd sell it and we'd split the proceeds four ways.

The last thing I needed was a lot on Kezar. When we'd moved to Washington, I'd sold the land on Horseshoe and the cabin on Kezar (the renters from Haverhill had made that decision much easier). I paid off all my loans and had $10,000 left over. Plus, I'd taken back a mortgage on the land on Horseshoe, which I'd restricted to one lot, so instead of paying out $80.90 a month, we were taking in $108.40. We had a nice home in Virginia. I was committed to my work at The Nature Conservancy, so we wouldn't be going back to New England, at least for a while. If we ever wanted a vacation on Kezar, we could rent from the Stone sisters. I called Mr. Severance and told him I wanted to sell Mom's lot.

"Can't," Mr. Severance said.

"Why not?" I asked, incredulous.

"Can't build on it. Lot's too small."

"How can that be? You sold it to us."

"That was back in sixty-three," he countered, "before the environmentalists pushed through all those new laws."

"What am I going to do?" I pleaded.

"Since your Mom's the original ownah, you might be able to get a variance. But the town won't give one to a newcomah."

I was stuck. Lots on Ladies Delight were selling for around $20,000, but it seemed the only way I could realize that value was to build something on the lot. That meant I'd have to come up with a plan, obtain all the permits, and find a builder. Supervising the construction of a cabin in Maine would be tough from D.C., but then I had a brainstorm.

In 1978, Ruth and I had adopted Don, a husky little six year old we'd taken in as a foster child. Don had had a rough life and we were determined to give him some pleasant memories, like the ones we had when we were growing up. Why spend a hot, sticky summer in Washington when we could be camping on the shores of Kezar? I had plenty of vacation time. If we had to build something, why not pitch a tent on Mom's lot and help build the cabin? That would be an experience to remember.

I went to the attic, pulled out Mom's trunk, and started weeding through her musty, mildewed plans. I finally settled on something she had called the Dollhouse. It was hand-sketched on a piece of graph paper and consisted of one main room with a loft, a little kitchen, and a bathroom. The dominant feature of the Dollhouse was the big fieldstone fireplace at one end. It reminded me of the de La Chapelle's fireplace, the one Rodney

Jordan had built. That had been ten years ago. Would Rodney still be in business?

There was only one Rodney Jordan listed in Bethel. I called the number and got Carol, his wife. "Rodney's not here," she told me. "He's working down to Severance Lodge." Carol gave me the number.

In the late seventies, Harold Severance had decided to convert his cabins from rentals to condominiums. He'd picked Rodney to be his head carpenter. When I got Rodney on the phone and told him I'd like to talk to him about building a cabin, he was noncommittal. As head carpenter at Severance Lodge, he had all the work he could handle. But just as I was about to hang up, Rodney said, "Might be able to do somethin' next summer. If ya're up this way, stop by and we can talk about it."

It appeared that if I wanted Rodney to be my builder, I'd have to pass inspection. I flew to Portland, rented a car, and drove to Lovell. I met Rodney at his shop just outside the entrance to Severance Lodge. He was leaning against his dented pickup. Rodney was a big man, at least six foot three, with a powerful upper body and huge, calloused hands. His rough, angular, weather-beaten face reminded me of a Maine fieldstone. I guessed that Rodney was crowding fifty, which put him a decade ahead of me, but there was a clarity in his bright blue eyes that made him seem much younger.

I didn't waste any words. "Could you build this cabin for me?" I said, unfolding Mom's plan.

Rodney spread the piece of graph paper over the hood of his pickup. He scratched his granite chin and gave me a studied look. "Ayuh. Didn't recognize the name over the phone, but I know these plans." He looked at me again. "Must've been ya mother showed 'em to me. Told her I could do it, but she never got back to me."

"She died," I said.

"Too bad," he said, picking up a twig. "She had good taste." Mom did have good taste, like Harold Severance. Mom always liked puttering past Severance Lodge because she said the cottages looked like little dollhouses. It was no coincidence that they'd both discovered Rodney.

"Well, will you build it?" I said.

"Reckon I could do it next summer," Rodney said, snapping the twig between his big fingers. "Gonna need a variance, though. Ayuh. Town meetin's not 'til March. Couldn't start 'til after the thaw anyway. That all right?"

"That's great," I said. Thanks to Mom, I'd passed inspection. Now I dropped the bomb. "Uh, there is one other thing. If it's all right with you, I'd like to help." Rodney didn't say anything. He fiddled with his twig and stared at the plans. I knew he was thinking it over. I was sure that no one at Severance Lodge ever asked him if they could help. "I don't want to take charge, or anything," I said. "I just want to be the gofer." Rodney still said nothing. "You know, a helper. The guy who fetches things, hands you nails and tools and stuff."

More silence. Finally Rodney looked up. "I guess that'd be all right," he said. "If ya're any good, ya'll save some money. If ya mess up, it'll cost ya some. Makes no difference to me."

When Ruth, Donald, Percy (our golden retriever), and I drove into Mom's lot the following July, Rodney was setting the last cinder block on the foundation. He nodded a noncommittal hello as we piled out. After meeting Ruth and Donald, Rodney watched with some interest as I began thrashing away at a patch of undergrowth next to the lake. I was eager to set up the new "expedition-quality" Eureka Deluxe tent that was to be our home for the next eight weeks. I'd spared no expense. The Eureka had a full-coverage fly, roll-up front door, reinforced corners, tube-type floor, and "all the ventilation and convenience money can buy in a family tent." It hadn't been easy selling Ruth on the concept that camping out for eight weeks on Mom's lot would be the ultimate family experience. Now I had to prove it.

My heart sank as a huge stack of premium-quality aluminum alloy poles joined together by high-grade shock cord tumbled onto the ground. They were followed by a waterproof nylon tent with top flies, mesh mosquito netting, mesh storage pockets, snap-on hooks, horseshoe zippers, and durable stay-put plastic stakes (all made in Korea, pole bag included). I picked up the long list of instructions. They might as well have been in Korean.

"Let's see," I said, "Tube A goes into Hinge D." I was totally unprepared for this sudden immersion in the world of high-tech camping. I should have given the Eureka a test pitch back home.

Ruth gave me one of her dubious looks. "Do you have any idea what you're doing?"

"Sure," I said with a false bravado. "Piece of cake. All I have to do is find Tube A and attach it to Hinge D."

Don had just turned nine, the age when sons first perceive that their fathers are not infallible. He sensed trouble. "Here, try this," he said, handing me a premium-quality aluminum alloy pole.

"Dammit, Don," I barked. "Don't touch anything."

"He was just trying to help," Ruth said.

"I don't need any help."

Ruth was getting ready to lay into me when we were interrupted. "Nice tent," Rodney said. He'd finished setting his block and had wandered over. "Mind if I look at it?"

"Please do," I said, hoping he would take over. He did.

"Better set up over here," he suggested. "We might need this space for lumber." Of course, Rodney's spot was much better than mine. Soon he had put the tent up, built a table out of some scrap wood, rearranged some stones into a fireplace, set some logs as chairs, produced a jug of water, started a fire, and shown me how to dig a latrine. By then, it was time for supper. "See ya in the mornin'," he said, climbing into his pickup. "We start at seven."

With our camp set up, we took a refreshing dip in the lake, cooked some Dinty Moore he-man stew over the fire, sat on Mom's rock, and watched the sun set into the White Mountains. As we crawled into our new L.L. Bean Deluxe Camp Bags with DuPont's Holofil II Fiber, "a multi-core insulation specially treated to offer enhanced resilience, loft, and comfort," I looked up through the top flies and thanked my lucky stars for Rodney. He'd gotten us off to a good start. As I closed my eyes and listened to the loons' eerie cries echo across the lake, my last thought was, this might actually work.

Percy was the first up. I'd wanted him to sleep outside, but Ruth and Don insisted that he sleep in the tent with us. He started barking just before the crash. I peeked out of my nylon mesh window and saw that a Hancock Lumber truck had just dumped a pile of lumber next to the new foundation. I groped for my watch. It read 6:45. They started early in Maine.

Rodney arrived promptly at seven. Not wanting to be late for my first day on the job, I slipped on my pants and hustled out to meet him. Ruth, Donald, and Percy were not so eager. They slept in. Rodney and I could have used some help sorting the lumber, but I didn't get them up. With eight weeks still to go in the Eureka, why press my luck.

By ten, when Rodney broke for coffee, we were ready to frame the floor. "Lay out them joists," Rodney told me. "I'll be back at one."

"Not 'til one?" I said, surprised. "That's some coffee break."

"Ayuh," said Rodney and drove off. I dutifully laid out the joists while Ruth, Donald, and Percy went for a swim.

Rodney was back at one. He explained our schedule while

we framed the floor. He still had plenty of work to do at Severance Lodge, but the guests at Severance didn't like to be disturbed before ten. Rodney would work at our place from seven to ten, then at Severance from ten to noon. His afternoons would be up for grabs. Sometimes he'd be at our place, sometimes he'd be at Severance, but there always would be plenty of work for me to do.

We soon got into a routine. Percy's bark would announce Rodney's arrival. I would roll out and go to work. Ruth would roll out and make a big breakfast. Don would roll out and run off to play with his new friends. Percy would roll out, eat most of Ruth's big breakfast, and go back to bed.

We weren't the only ones in a routine. As Rodney pointed out, there was a myriad of wildlife that had also settled into their summer schedule. A mink who lived in the base of a hollow tree along the shore would be the first out fishing each morning. Initially she went out alone. Then, as the summer progressed, she was followed by her string of kits.

Next up would be the red squirrels, chattering and dropping nuts from way up in the oaks. They put in long days. They knew they had to hustle to collect and store all the nuts they'd need for the long, cold winter. Chipmunks, with their tails straight up like periscopes and their jowls bulging with booty, would scurry back and forth, hiding nuts here and there. A kingfisher would fly along the shoreline, looping from branch to branch, his big head always searching for a fish. The kingfisher was Ruth's favorite. She liked his spirit and zip.

As the day wore on, a pair of Canada geese would paddle into the cove with their fuzzy brown goslings. They'd be followed by a blue-winged teal and her new ducklings. At first there were eight, then six, then four, and finally three. "Needs eight to get three," Rodney explained. "Ayuh. Hawks, owls, pickerel, bass, turtles have to eat, too."

The loons were unpredictable. They had no set routine. We'd see them patrolling their territory, sometimes with a chick on their back, and hear their eerie cries anytime day or night. My favorite critter was the fox. We'd only see it at night, when we were coming back from the drive-in theater. It would be hunting in the field at the end of the road, pouncing on mice or sniffing around where I'd seen a mother grouse and her brood. Like teal, grouse need a brood to survive.

Rodney's wife, Carol, would usually come about nine. She'd have a cup of coffee with Ruth and make a list of what Rodney needed. Carol served as Rodney's helper and business manager. She ordered the materials, ran the errands, did most of the painting, and paid the bills. Carol was punctual and precise—my weekly statements were always plumb to the penny—plus she kept Rodney working. Rodney was not the typical taciturn Mainer. He was always stopping work to tell me why a certain rock was formed this way, or why a certain board bent that way, or why some animal was running, swimming, or flying past us at that moment. I was happy to listen. It was Carol who'd tell Rodney, "Stop ya yakkin' and get back to work."

All sorts of people would drop by to see Rodney. They'd start by talking business, but soon the conversation would lapse into hunting, fishing, and other matters of great importance. My favorite was Leon. Leon was part owner of Hancock Lumber, and his own best salesman. Rodney liked to spread his business around, but Leon wanted it all. Leon would park his pickup next to the lumber pile, get out, and start inspecting every beam and board for the Hancock brand. When he found a stray, he'd confront Rodney. "What did Asa charge ya for this two-by-eight?"

"Thirty-nine cents per foot." Rodney didn't have to ask how Leon knew he'd bought the two-by-eight from Asa. Leon knew the lineage of every timber in Oxford County.

"Could've given it to ya for thirty-five."

"Hell, Leon, ya quoted me forty-three last week."

"Just went on sale." Then Leon would look at me and shake his head. "Too bad."

And so it went. When Leon had finished his business, he would grab Donald's ball and glove and insist on showing us his four best pitches. Leon claimed to have been a big-league prospect. He was still the number one man in the Hancock Lumber team's rotation, which, according to Leon, was the most feared in all of western Maine. All work would stop while Leon showcased his stuff. It was immediately obvious to me that what Leon had gained in girth, he'd lost in zip. "Good thing ya own the business," Rodney would tell him. "If ya didn't, they'd have ya out in right field."

After four weeks, the cottage was framed and under roof. It was time to start the fireplace. With its massive chimney, the fireplace would be the heart of the cabin, and building it was a project for the entire family. Donald and I would collect the rocks. Ruth would help Rodney set them.

Collecting the rocks was no easy job. The chimney was to be six feet wide and three feet deep. It eventually would rise twenty feet. That required a lot of rocks. "Take the pickup," Rodney told us. "Drive back into the woods and strip 'em off old walls. Choose different sizes. Get a nice mix."

It sounded simple, but Rodney had neglected to tell us about the yellow jackets. Don and I paid dearly for those rocks. The third day out, we hit our first nest. They caught us totally by surprise. I'd thrown a rock down to Don, who was going to pick it up and put it in the truck. It had landed right on top of a nest. Don was stung nine times. I was a little quicker; they only got me five. After that, Don wouldn't get out of the truck, and I couldn't blame him.

While Don and I were busy dodging swarms of yellow jackets, Ruth and Rodney were having a great time. Ruth was the mortar maid. Her job was to scrape the excess mortar off a rock once Rodney set it. Ruth and Rodney hardly noticed when Don and I pulled in with a new load of rocks. They were too busy discussing the world according to Rodney. Rodney had extraordinary practical knowledge and Ruth was loaded with education, so they were always engaged in some deep discussion. I was a little miffed that they weren't getting more done. Our rocks were piling up, but the chimney was rising at the tedious rate of only two feet per day. When I asked Rodney why they weren't moving faster, he explained, "Two feet a day's all she can hold. Takes a day for the mortar to set up. Any more than that, she'll collapse of her own weight."

Don and I would line up each new load of rocks at the base of the chimney. Rodney would survey them from above. "Hand me that one," he'd say, pointing to a rock with his trowel.

"Hah," I'd scoff. "That'll never fit. It's too big." Or too small, or too round, or too flat, or whatever. Rodney would ignore my analysis, take the stone, cradle it in his big hands, and gently set it into place.

Usually Rodney was right, but every once in a while, one wouldn't fit. "Hah. What did I tell you? Try this one," I'd say, holding up my selection.

Still ignoring me, Rodney would hold his rock out in front of him and talk to it for a while. "Now come on, don't be difficult," he'd say. "This's just the place for ya."

Once the man from Bethel had spoken, he'd anoint the rock with a dab of mortar and glide it into place, a perfect fit. While Ruth scraped away the excess mortar, Rodney would look down at me with a beatific smile. "How's she look?" Stung again, I'd retreat for more rocks.

Rodney capped the chimney the day before we had to leave. That evening, he and Carol came to dinner to celebrate. He set up a grill in the new fireplace and put on some moose steaks.

While they cooked, we all sat down by Mom's rock, soaked in the view, and watched the sun set into the White Mountains. Now that Mom's cabin was done, I had no intention of ever selling it. There was too much of us in it. These memories were worth any price.

"We did all right," I said to Rodney.

"Ayuh."

"And what about our deal? Remember what you said? If I worked out, I'd save some money. If I screwed up, I'd lose some?"

"Ayuh."

"Well, how'd I do?"

"Been thinkin' about it," he said, stroking his big granite chin. "Figure ya broke about even."

I think Rodney was kidding, but maybe not. In any event, I didn't argue with him. Looking back on our summer and all that we'd learned, I knew we'd done a lot better than just breaking even.

MY LAST HURRAH

Softball is special in Lovell. From June through September, there's a game every Thursday night at Westways. These days, Westways is one of the plushest resorts on Kezar Lake, but in the early 1900s it was the estate of William Armstrong Fairburn, the man who made Diamond Match. According to a publication put out by Diamond Match, "William Armstrong Fairburn was a man who had a great love of the outdoors and sports."

This love is evident at Westways. It has a bowling alley, tennis court, card room, and grand boathouse. But the jewel of Billy Fairburn's summer setting is the little diamond he cut amongst the towering pines and white birches. Fairburn's field looks over the entire Upper Bay and into the White Mountains. It's a great place to play ball.

To the casual observer, the Thursday night game might seem unworthy of the setting. There are no teams, no uniforms, no umpires, no list of rules, and no restrictions on who can play. It's a game with little polish, played mostly by locals who don't care how they look, or even who wins. They come out on Thursday nights to have a good time.

Although seldom asked, summer folk, especially those staying at Westways, are welcome to play. I'd heard about Thursday night softball from Bob Drew, the electrician who was wiring our cabin. Bob spied my glove and asked if I wanted to play. I was flattered. To the best of my knowledge, Stephen King and I are the only summer folk to receive such an invitation, and Stephen King's a Mainard. Like Stephen, I immediately accepted.

There's no confusing the Thursday night softballers with the guests at Westways. Around five P.M., battered pickups start pulling in under the trees beyond right field. Guys wearing paint-spattered pants and tattered T-shirts emerge with their coolers and gloves and make their way to the bench. Many have a cigarette dangling from their lips. Most are sucking down a beer. They're carpenters, painters, caretakers, plumbers, electricians, and woodsmen. Every one of them has just come from a long, hard day's work. Westways does well to let these men use its field one night a week. They deserve it.

When enough players show up, two senior softballers quietly step aside to pick the teams. Once the teams are selected, the pickers walk along the bench and tell you if you're "in" or "out," at bat or in the field. It's a wonderful system. No one knows for sure where he's drafted. I like to fancy myself as being one of the top choices, although that's hardly the case given all the good ballplayers in Lovell. I am fairly confident I'm picked before Stephen King. If someone kept statistics at Westways, Steve's batting average would look like a real horror story.

Nobody's assigned a position; you evolve into the lineup. Dan McLaughlin always plays left. Mark Tripp automatically heads for first. John Bliss owns third. Paul Armington stops at short. Hopie likes to climb the mound. Newcomers usually end up in right field or at second.

It took me a couple of years, but I evolved into a catcher. I like catching because it gives me some control, albeit very little, over the lack of mental discipline that pervades Thursday night softball. Fundamentals like throwing ahead of the runner, hitting the cutoff man, or going for a base hit rather than the fence when a runner's in scoring position are not part of the Thursday night game. As catcher, I can shout out situations such as "Runners at first and second, two outs, play at any base" or "Man at first, no outs, let's go for two," but nobody ever listens. Everyone does just what he wants.

I wince every time a ball is hit to Steven Bennett in center. Steven has a slingshot for an arm and is quite proud of it. He likes to rifle the ball home, no matter what. Even if someone is just trying to stretch a single into a double, Steve inevitably uncorks a hummer towards the plate. It frequently flies over the backstop into the woods. No one seems to mind that the runner ends up at third. "Nice arm, Steve" is all I hear as I plow through the poison ivy trying to find the ball.

Freddy Wilson is another young, undisciplined talent. Despite muscles on top of muscles, Freddy has a naturally smooth stroke. He's a lefty who could hit for a great average, but nobody at Westways cares about Freddy's average, least of all Freddy. All Freddy ever wants to do is put another dent in somebody's pickup. Anything parked under the trees beyond right field is fair game. Who cares if the score's tied, the bases loaded, and all he needs is a single to win. Freddy's going for the pickups, and there's universal merriment when he nails one. The louder the clang, the more they love it. Freddy prances around the bases, beaming his boyish smile. "Who'd he hit?" someone asks." "Got Owen's Chevy, right on the hood." Everyone hoots and hollers at Owen. "Hope you're insured." "What's the difference? Won't notice one more dent on that wreck."

Like Freddy, William Armstrong Fairburn must have fancied

himself a home run hitter. He built his tennis court in left center, just close enough to tempt any rightie. Lifting one over the fence into the court is the delight of every Thursday night softballer. After three courtless seasons, it became my obsession.

I'd lost whatever power I had when I broke my wrist in high school. Rather than going for the fence, I have to be content to dump the ball into left, right, or center. For two years the locals must have assumed that the reason I never went deep was that I was some old has-been trying to maintain my average. During my third season, they wised up. Dan McLaughlin was the first to figure it out. "Move up. This guy's got no power," he'd yell from left to Steven Bennett in center and to whoever was playing right.

It got embarrassing. I could no longer dump in a single, and whenever I swung for the court, it was an easy pop to left or center. Even Angelo Campo, a rotund Italian who looks like a short Fidel Castro, started playing me up. The final blow came one night when Stephen King popped a grand slam into the court. After that, I could no longer fancy myself as a top draft. There was no question in my mind about who was being chosen last. I had to develop some offensive punch.

That winter, I bought myself a running machine and some weights. "Now that I'm forty-five," I told Ruth, "I'm going to whip myself back into shape." That was a lie. What I really was going to do was make myself strong enough to put a softball into the tennis court at Westways.

The next summer, just before we left for Maine, I went to see my optometrist. I knew I needed new glasses, but up to now I'd resisted. I was afraid that the next change would push me into bifocals. Sure enough. "You need bifocals," my optometrist said.

"No," I replied. "What I need is a pair of hitting glasses. I want the same vision as Ted Williams, twenty-fifteen." The optometrist fixed me up with a pair of beauties. They looked like the Hubble telescope. I couldn't read the headlines of the *Portland Press Herald,* but I could count the stitches on a softball at forty-five feet.

The new me showed up early at Westways on the first Thursday in July. I was ready to start my fourth season. Besides my cooler and glove, I was carrying my new bat, thirty-three inches of solid ash painted red with white lettering that read "Ball Buster." I sat on the bench pretending not to notice the appraising looks of that night's pickers, Tom McLaughlin, the first selectman of Lovell, and Eddie Nista, the chairman of the planning commission, and announced the new me by casually crushing my beer can with one hand. I felt as strong as Freddy Wilson.

It had been raining all day, but the sun had come out right at five. Unfortunately, a lot of the guys hadn't. At 5:30, there were only fourteen of us, or seven a side. "Dave, you're out," Eddie said, as he and Tom moved down the bench setting their teams. "How about playing left until Dan gets here." What could I say? Catcher was the most expendable position. I dutifully trotted to left.

I was treading hallowed ground, and I knew it. Dan McLaughlin was the best player ever to grace William Armstrong Fairburn's little diamond. Of the five things a ballplayer must do—run, field, throw, hit, and hit for power—Dan did them all better than anybody at Westways. Dan McLaughlin was the Ted Williams of Thursday night softball, a natural. Nobody was ever going to look at left field and mistake me for Dan.

Hopie was first up. The batting order always went pitcher, catcher, first, second, third, short, then around the outfield. That meant Hopie was pitching. Hopie was a hippie, a throwback to the sixties. He still had a big bushy beard, and what was left of his hair was tied back in a ponytail. There wasn't a competitive bone in his body. He was notorious for serving up meatballs. I couldn't wait to let the Ball Buster launch one of his servings into the court.

Hopie went for the first pitch, looping a little Texas Leaguer to left. Dan would have had it in his pocket. It was going to be a stretch for me. Thanks to my Ted Williams eyes, I got a good jump and sprinted in for the catch. It looked like a shoestringer, but I was going to make it. I could almost read the label as the ball floated toward my outstretched glove. I saw it snow-cone in the webbing just as someone screamed, "Look out!"

I had no idea where I was, but I could hear people talking. "He's coming to," someone said. Slowly, I opened my eyes. A large group was gathered around me. My vision was blurred, but I could see Paul McLaughlin standing over me. Paul was Dan and Tom's baby brother. At six foot three and easily 250 pounds, Paul was one big baby. He was playing short and had been coming out for the ball when we met. "Gee, I'm awful sorry," he said. "You okay? Gawd, I only bumped ya."

I tried to answer but couldn't. There was no air in my lungs. I couldn't catch my breath. John Bliss grabbed me by the belt and started jerking me up and down. John is the local surveyor, but he looks like Rusty Jones, the character who used to keep your car from rusting. He was just the combination I needed, someone who could help me find my bearings and refurbish my body. "Go easy!" someone shouted. "You might give 'im a haht attack." John ignored the warning and kept bouncing me up and down.

Finally, I felt the air come rushing back into my lungs. When they were full, I sat up, very slowly. "Here's ya glasses," someone said. I put the Hubbles back on. They were bent but still intact. Next to me, lying on the ground, was the ball. Damn, I'd dropped it.

Mike Ackerly, a flatlander from Long Island, helped me back to the bench. During the commotion, Dan McLaughlin had shown up and was back in left. Play resumed as I sucked down a couple of beers and watched.

In the bottom of the sixth, with two away, Eddie Nista asked me if I'd like to hit. Freddy Wilson had just put a new dent in Bob Drew's van. There'd been two on, so Eddie's team had a comfortable lead.

I adjusted the Hubbles, picked out the Ball Buster, and tottered to the plate. The opposition moved in. Angelo was practically in the infield. I stepped out of the batter's box, rubbed some dirt in my hands, and looked at the court. It was now or never. I stepped back into the box knowing I could do it. Hopie served up a particularly tender meatball. I rocked back on my heels, took my best cut, and watched in dismay as the ball dribbled to a stop just in front of the mound. Hopie picked it up and threw to first. I hobbled back to the bench and got myself another beer.

"Nice try," Eddie said. "You'll get 'em next time."

"Yeah, thanks," I said, but I knew I wouldn't.

The sun was dropping behind the White Mountains, setting on my softball career. I decided not to stay for the seventh inning. I was beginning to hurt all over. I picked up my cooler and my glove, restraightened the Hubbles, and took a long last look at William Armstrong Fairburn's diamond. Twenty guys wearing paint-spattered pants and tattered T-shirts were all enjoying themselves, but it was time for me to go.

ABSOLUTE LOONACY

Kezar, like most lakes in southern Maine, is no longer very wild. It suffers from too many cottages (mine included), too many people, too many big boats, and now even a couple of Jet Skis, the latest and loudest insult to anything wild. But Kezar does have its loons, and every year they keep coming back.

It has been reported that in all of neighboring New Hampshire, with its 156 lakes and ponds, the summer population of loons does not exceed four hundred. Some days in July, I've counted as many as nineteen loons on Kezar, and in fall when they raft up, that number can easily double. A softballer I play with claims that he once saw fifty-four loons swimming in the Upper Bay, but he told me this after a few beers, so I put a mental asterisk next to that sighting.

Most people in Lovell are proud of Kezar and want to protect what's left of its natural beauty. The Kezar Lake Association is very active. Every year it distributes a brochure outlining the dos and don'ts of Kezar. The loons are responsible for a lot of the don'ts. Don't chase them, don't harm them, don't disturb them, don't interfere with them, and don't bother them in any way.

One well-known story is that when Hollywood came to the Northeast looking for a place to shoot *On Golden Pond,* its first choice was Kezar. But the Kezar Lake Association didn't want anybody upsetting its loons, so Hollywood had to settle for Squam Lake in New Hampshire.

The pair down at our end of the Lower Bay often feeds in front of our cabin. We never take them for granted, but they are pretty common, so I was somewhat surprised one afternoon when Ruth suddenly called, "David, come quick! Look at the loons!" I rushed out onto the porch and saw something thrashing about in the brush right at the shoreline. I'd never seen a loon in that close, and what made it even more amazing was that our neighbors, Andy and Marge Koop, were out swimming not thirty feet away. Wild loons just don't get that close to people, not even people as nice as the Koops.

Don was down on the dock working on his boat. "Hey, Don! Look at the loons," I yelled. If Don saw them, he didn't seem to care. "Dave, can you bring me a wrench?" was all he said.

The loons started to shriek. The Koops stopped swimming. My first thought was that the loons had cornered an exceptionally large and tasty school of fish. What else could make them come so close to humans and the shore? What a break. Most of my time at The Nature Conservancy was spent dealing with lawyers and landowners, but here was nature on my very doorstep. I felt privileged to be able to share this unique moment with my family. "Don!" I shouted. "Stop fooling with your boat and look at the loons."

Don was fifteen, and nature was not on the top of his communing list. He remained preoccupied with his boat. "Dave, you could probably see them a lot better from down here. And when you come, how about bringing me that wrench?"

Don was right. I was too far away to see the loons clearly. I ran to the dock, without the wrench. When I got there, I saw two loons dive not more than twenty feet from me. While I stared at the cove waiting for them to surface, two streams of air bubbles came streaking under the dock. Two loons popped up right on the far side of Don's boat. They weren't fishing. They were trying to kill each other. The larger one had the smaller one by the neck and was forcing its head under the water. I could see blood.

Finally, Don was interested. "Dave, what are you going to do?"

I didn't know what to do. I couldn't just stand there and watch one loon kill another. On the other hand, was it right to interfere with Nature? Survival of the fittest and all that good stuff? What would the Kezar Lake Association say? I made a quick decision. To hell with Darwin. I didn't want this loon on my conscience.

I leaped off the dock into the shallows. The aggressor saw me coming and released his grip for an instant. That was all the little guy needed. He burst free and beat his way around the point. The big guy took off after him. They were both screaming bloody murder. I stood there, scared and confused, like the first person at the scene of a horrible accident.

The lots on the point are undeveloped, and the shoreline is still well hidden by bushes and trees. I sloshed out of the water through the undergrowth towards the sound of more thrashing, splashing, and screaming. I stumbled over a boulder, and there at the water's edge directly at my feet were the two loons. The big one again had the smaller bird's neck in his beak and was forcing its head under the water. Again, I didn't know what to do. I could have bent over and pulled them apart, but up this close, these loons looked very big, and the bigger one looked very upset.

I leaned over and waved my arms to signal a TKO, a technical knock out. "All right, you guys, break it up!" I said. Remarkably, the big loon let go and paddled back to a neutral corner. I expected the little guy to make another break for freedom, but instead, and I swear this is the truth, he waddled between my legs and cowered into the bank. I have probably read more articles about loons than there are loons on Kezar Lake, but nothing I have ever read prepared me for this situation. Here I was, standing on the shoreline with one loon howling at me from not more than ten feet away, while the other one, a completely wild bird, hid between my legs. I could have bent over and picked him up without taking a step.

Now what? It was obvious that the larger loon wasn't going to quit, and the other one wasn't about to leave my protection. I wasn't going to pick up the small one, because he wasn't all that small and had a very large and very sharp beak. The only solution seemed to be to drive away the big guy. But how? Yelling might further upset the bird at my feet. Maybe I could throw some pebbles at the larger bird. But there weren't any pebbles, only rocks the size of my head. Those would never do.

Then I remembered Don. "Hey, Don, get your boat over here, quick!" I yelled.

"I can't. I need the wrench."

That wasn't what I wanted or needed to hear. "Get that boat over here right now, or I'll wrench you."

After what sounded like some muffled unpleasantries, I heard Don's motor start. He came chugging around the point. When he saw my predicament, even Don was impressed. "Gee, Dave, how did you get so close to that loon?"

"I didn't get close to him. He got close to me. Now get your boat in here and back this other loon off." I must have sounded pretty authoritative, because Don gave me one of his infrequent "yes, sirs." Slowly he nosed his boat between me and the larger loon. The bird reluctantly turned away from the shore, and Don gently herded him down the lake.

With the big bird out of the way, I turned my attention to the poor guy nestled at my feet. Its head was hidden in a clump of grass. I could see it was cut on the neck, but not too badly. It was breathing heavily but seemed all right. I figured the best thing to do was to leave it alone for half an hour and see what happened. If it hadn't moved by then, I'd call somebody from the Kezar Lake Association.

As I made my way back to the cabin, I was very pleased with myself. I had saved a loon from certain destruction. What more could a conservationist ask of himself? This positive feeling was positively reinforced when I saw an attractive young woman in an equally attractive bikini standing outside my porch. Ah, I thought, no good deed goes unrewarded. I sucked in my tummy, pumped up my chest, and strode forward prepared to receive my well-deserved plaudits.

That was a mistake. In her hand, the young woman held a Kezar Lake Association brochure. Before I could introduce myself, she said accusingly, "Is that your son out there in that boat?"

"Yes."

"Then I'm citing you for harassing a loon," she said, thrusting the brochure at me. "We have very strict rules about harassing loons on Kezar Lake."

Citing me? I was flabbergasted. Here I was, expecting the Order of Audubon, and I end up getting cited, whatever that meant. "Citing? Me? Miss, I don't think you understand. I just saved a loon. One was trying to kill the other."

She was not convinced. "I saw those loons. They came right by my beach. They were mating."

Mating? I thought to myself, if this is her idea of sex, I'm glad I'm middle-aged and married. But I didn't say that. What I did say was, "Mating? The mating season's long gone. Those two loons were having a territorial fight."

At this point, Ruth, who was still on the porch watching this fiasco, rose to my defense. "He's right," she said. "He helped finance a loon study."

The "he" Ruth referred to, of course, was not me personally but The Nature Conservancy. In 1984, I'd initiated a study of a massive loon die-off (at least five hundred birds) around Dog Island in Florida. But since the debate with this young woman was still up in the air, Ruth had wisely decided to leave the Conservancy out of it. What if I was wrong?

The young woman hesitated. At that moment, I knew I had her. I quickly pressed my advantage. "I sincerely appreciate your concern, but I think I have the situation pretty well under control. I'm letting one loon rest in the weeds over there, and I think my son has coaxed the other loon far enough away so it'll no longer be a problem."

It worked. Much to my relief, she seemed placated. We moved on to introductions and who-do-you-knows. It turned out that she was the daughter of Mr. Perry, the former owner of the marina. I told her how we had bought our canoe from him twenty years earlier. After a very friendly discussion, she departed with her brochure. I went back to check on my loon and was further relieved to find that it had regained its composure and returned to the wild.

The next day, I attended the dedication of a virgin forest in northern New Hampshire given to The Nature Conservancy by Champion International, the big paper company. By chance, Tudor Richards, president of the New Hampshire Audubon Society and a recognized expert on loons, was on the speaker's platform with me. After the ceremony, I pulled Tudor aside and told him my story. At its conclusion, I asked him, "Well, Tudor, was I right? Was it territorial or were they mating?"

Tudor put on a wistful look. "Oh, territorial by all means. I would have given anything to be there," he said. "You didn't by any chance take a picture, did you?"

I was vindicated. But still, I decided to restrict my conservation efforts to lawyers and landowners. I know how to deal with them. Nature's a different story. In the future, I'll leave the loons to Tudor Richards and the Kezar Lake Association.

GOLFING WITH THE BISHOP

I'm not much of a golfer. I only play a couple of rounds a year, and even then I usually call it quits after nine holes. Nine holes is plenty for me, especially since nine holes is all my opponent, the Bishop, cares to play.

The Right Reverend George Leslie Cadigan is the same age as my father, but I consider him more of a friend than a father. In addition to our mediocre golf games, the Bishop and I have other things in common. We're both married to Wellesley women, we're both committed to conservation, and we both played football for Amherst.

It was conservation that brought us together. Right after I started working for The Nature Conservancy, George called wanting help with a project in Lovell. At the time, George was the Episcopal Bishop of Missouri. He and his wife, Jane, had a place on Kezar, and George was heading a project committee that was trying to preserve Sucker Brook, the outlet to Horse-shoe Pond. Naturally, I'd heard of the Bishop. Everyone who played for Amherst knew about George Leslie Cadigan, the outstanding halfback and captain of the '32 team that almost beat Princeton. Based on the Bishop's reputation, the Conservancy bought the land and George and his committee quickly raised the money. The Bishop's spirit and commitment have been the heart and soul of conservation in Lovell.

While it was conservation that brought us together, it was competition that cemented our friendship. George hates to lose. I find it amusing that a bishop is so openly competitive, but George is a great athlete and all great athletes hate to lose. As he often reminds me when we're discussing Amherst, "The thirty-two team would have been undefeated were it not for Princeton."

That loss was not George's fault. In fact, he almost stole the game from the bigger and more talented Tigers. "Back in thirty-two," he tells me, "the length of the game was determined by the captains. It was an extremely hot day when we played Princeton in Palmer Stadium. Just before the coin toss, I suggested to Josh Billings, Princeton's captain, that the heat might be too much for some of Princeton's older alumni and it would be better for them if we played shorter halves. Josh, being a gentleman and concerned about Princeton's older alumni, agreed."

When Josh Billings came back to Princeton's well-stocked bench and announced that he'd agreed to cut the length of the game, Fritz Chrysler (Princeton's coach and the same Fritz Chrysler who later turned Michigan into a perennial powerhouse) nearly swallowed his whistle. Amherst had arrived with only twenty-three men; Princeton had more than ninety. Fritz Chrysler knew right away that George Cadigan, that kind, caring kid from Amherst, had already made the biggest play of the game.

"We played them even for three quarters," George says wistfully, "but then we ran out of steam. Princeton was undefeated that year: national champs. If only I'd clipped Josh for a few more minutes, we might have won."

Although he won't admit it, I suspect that George keeps a list of friends he likes to beat at golf. Most of them are old cronies whose best drives are far behind them. Due to my age, I'm the only tiger left on the Bishop's schedule. If he can beat me, he's almost guaranteed an undefeated season. For that reason, I know that before the summer's over, I'll get a call from George suggesting that we play a round of golf. "Just the two of us," he'll say. "It'll give us a chance to talk."

The match is always at the Kezar Lake Country Club, George's home course, but there's little chance for us to talk. As we make our way to the first tee, the Bishop is too busy introducing me to everybody. "Good afternoon, Louise," George says to the lady behind the counter. "Louise is from the oldest family in Lovell," the Bishop informs me. "I remember the day she was born." I nod respectfully. Louise clearly enjoys the recognition.

As we make our way through the crowd gathered around the first tee, the Bishop's hand is in perpetual motion. "This fellow's daughter is number one in her class at Bowdoin," he announces. The fellow smiles proudly. "This lady's son just joined the navy." The lady beams. The Bishop grabs a little roly-poly guy and punches him on the arm. "Hutch owns the best dairy farm in all of Maine," he tells me. "And he's got the most pull in Lovell."

I chuckle at the Bishop's little joke. Everyone chuckles at the Bishop's little joke. I can tell that they're wondering how I get to play golf with the Bishop. His next introduction answers that question. "David, here, was a great athlete at Amherst," he shouts to an old codger with a hearing aid. "Watch him hit the ball, It'll go a mile." Everyone nods. They all know the Bishop is gung-ho Amherst.

When it's our turn to tee off, George offers me the honor. I politely decline. I'm wise to his strategy. Having just introduced me as a great golfer, which, of course, I'm not, he's now putting the pressure on me to prove it.

The Bishop holds out a fist. "Odds or evens?"

"Evens," I say. He opens his fist. There are two tees.

"You win. You're up!" he says, overjoyed that I've been so lucky. Since I won, I should have the choice, but who's going to argue with the Bishop.

I watch in disgust as my drive dribbles off the tee. Much to the delight of his flock, the Bishop smacks a beauty, 175 yards right down the middle. I know I'm in trouble. The first hole is only 292 yards, an easy par four for the Bishop, especially if he bangs a big drive. Today I'm lucky. I escape with a halve when the Bishop's putter lets him down on what should have been a gimme. I give the Bishop nothing.

The second hole, a tricky par four, plays to my advantage. The tee overlooks a bog. Even a good golfer needs a respectable poke to reach the fairway. The Bishop no longer has enough power to clear the bog. His only shot is to punch the ball between two pine trees and hope it runs past the ladies' tee. I know that if I can clear the bog, I'll have him.

It's still my honor. I feel a surge of confidence as I tee up my ball. I picture myself striding manfully down the fairway while the Bishop has to humbly walk over to the ladies' tee. The Bishop can see I'm on top of my game. Without his flock to distract me, he tries a different gambit. "Did you hear that Evergreen Valley's been sold again?" he announces during my practice swing. I can feel my muscles stiffen. George and I serve on the local land trust together, and Evergreen Valley is a major development that has been a constant thorn in our sides. If it ever took off, it would wreck much of Kezar's natural ambiance.

I hate Evergreen Valley, and the Bishop knows it. My drive nose-dives into the muck.

"Too bad," he says as he tees up his ball. His drive reminds me of a camel making its way through the eye of a needle. It brushes the branches of one pine, bounces underneath another, skips past the ladies' tee, and rolls neatly to the edge of the fairway. "It'll play," he says cheerfully.

I take an "X" after hacking my way out of the bog, into a trap, over the green, and back into another trap. George has parlayed a nice three-wood into a bogey. "Dave, you mustn't worry about Evergreen Valley," he tells me on our way to the third tee. "I think the land trust might have a chance to acquire it, and I'm sure we can raise the money." It's easy for the Bishop to be optimistic. He's one up.

I've heard that the real pros intentionally fade their shots into the crowd. That way, if a shot gets away from them, it might hit a fan and bounce back into play. The Bishop is a real pro. On the third hole, a gentle par four dogleg to the left, he always plays into the drainage ditch. That gives him a free lift and an easy five iron to the green. I watch in disgust as his drive dutifully disappears into the ditch. Fortunately, the thought of the land trust buying Evergreen Valley has calmed me. I regain my composure, and we halve the third with matching pars.

The fourth is surrounded by majestic pines; it is George's favorite hole. He claims that it reminds him of a cathedral. I wince at the reference. "It amuses me that some people believe I get a lucky bounce just because I'm a Bishop," he says as he kneels reverently to tee up his ball.

"Heaven forbid," I say as his dubbed drive miraculously hits the cart track and bounds straight down the nave. I slice my ball into the south transept. The Bishop is on in two. My second shot ends up behind the organ. The Bishop gives thanks for another par, while I confess to a six. We exit the cathedral with me two down.

The fifth hole is a little par three, a simple seven iron over a pond. Concentration is the key. It's here that George likes to run his "Josh Billings" play. It's here that he likes to talk his opponent out of the match. "Is Ruth's mother coming up this year?" he asks innocently.

The Bishop knows that Ruth's mother would never come to Maine. During the summer, Ruth's mother expects us to come to the Jersey Shore. That's where Ruth went before I came along, and that's where she wants Ruth now. I try to concentrate, but all I can think about is my poor mother-in-law, sitting alone on the boardwalk, gazing out at an empty sea as the sun rises and sets over the Jersey Shore. The scene is shattered by a splash as my ball plops into the pond. So much for the fifth.

We halve the sixth, but I'm still three down with only three holes to go. I need a miracle, and it arrives on the seventh. The seventh is a long par three, and like most par threes it gets backed up. Some kids are teeing off when we walk up. I can tell from their T-shirts, jeans, sneakers, and garish hats that they're locals. A woman is with them, obviously a mother. A beatific glow sweeps over her when she sees the Bishop. "Oh, Bishop Cadigan," she says in a heavy Maine accent, "I'm so-and-so's daughtah."

I don't recognize the name, but of course the Bishop does. "Oh, so-and-so's daughter," he says. "So nice to see you. How are your parents?"

"They're doin' just fine. Dad's same as evah, and mum's still puttin' up with him."

"Wonderful, wonderful," the Bishop says. Then he remembers me. "Dave, here, has a place on the Lower Bay. He was a great athlete at Amherst. He probably could have been a pro golfer if he had started at the age of these young fellows."

The woman looks at me as if I were Arnold Palmer. "Nice to meet ya," she says.

"Which one is your boy?" the Bishop asks.

The woman points to a wiry little towhead. "That's mine on the right. But the one hittin' the ball, that's Ed Larrabee's boy."

The Bishop perks up at the mention of Ed Larrabee. For many years, Ed was the groundskeeper at the Kezar Lake Country Club. He's an old friend of the Bishop's. We watch as little Ed pounds his tee shot deep into the woods. He rips off his red-white-and-blue Budweiser hat, throws it on the ground, and stomps on it. The Bishop steps forward to greet him. Little Ed is taken by surprise. The Bishop immediately tries to put him at ease. "Why, Ed," he says reassuringly, "my, how you've grown."

Like most teenagers, Little Ed is uncomfortable meeting an adult, especially after just having stomped his hat into the ground. "Ayuh," he says, studying his sneakers.

Undaunted, the Bishop continues. "Please give my very best to your parents."

Little Ed shuffles. "Ayuh."

"Please tell them that you met George Cadigan."

Little Ed looks up as if to say, George who?

"That's George Cadigan," the Bishop repeats. "They'll know me; I married your sister."

Little Ed gives the Bishop a strange look. He knows his brother-in-law, and it sure ain't the Bishop. Little Ed reaches down, snaps up his hat, jumps into his cart, and speeds away towards the woods. His friends run after him, laughing. "That's the guy who married your sister?" one yells. "She sure did pick an old one!" The woman is clearly embarrassed. "Nice to meet ya," she says to me as she scurries down the path.

The Bishop is speechless. I've never seen him flummoxed. He's so discombobulated that I steal the next two holes. If I can win the ninth, I'll claim a draw, which for me is as good as a win since it would put an asterisk next to the Bishop's undefeated season.

The ninth is the longest hole on the course, a 524-yard killer. It's hot, and George is sweating. Being thirty-four years his junior, I, like Princeton, should be able to run him into the ground. But the Bishop isn't about to fold. Like all great athletes, he comes up with a little something extra.

"I talked to the coach this morning. He says we're in for a tough season."

The coach, of course, is Jim Ostendarp, head football coach at Amherst. "So what?" I say, addressing my ball. "The coach always says we're in for a tough season."

"No, no," the Bishop protests. "This year he means it."

"How can he mean it?" I say, taking a practice swing. "I thought we were loaded."

"Oh, you haven't heard? Our quarterback is taking his junior year abroad," the Bishop says, shaking his head. "Bowdoin, Middlebury, Wesleyan, Tufts, Trinity, and, of course, Williams all look much stronger. We'll be lucky to take Colby."

This is bad news. I've never heard the Bishop talk this way. It's his optimism that usually counters the coach's pessimism. If George says we're in trouble, then we're in trouble. I try to focus on my shot, but visions of Polar Bears, Panthers, Cardinals, Jumbos, Bantams, and, of course, Purple Cows all feasting on Lord Jeffrey is too much. My grip tightens. The ball shrinks to the size of a pea. I jerk my driver into the air and flail away. The head of the club buries itself in the ground a good six inches behind the ball. I watch in disgust as my drive trickles over the edge of the tee.

"Well, you're in the fairway," the Bishop says, regaining his old optimism. He's fully recovered and it shows. He slams his best drive of the day.

Is it really possible that the Lord Jeffs could get kicked by the Mules? I flog my second shot into a trap. The Bishop strokes another beauty. For an octogenarian, he's hitting the ball a mile. His third shot will put him within easy reach of the green. I've lost my advantage. There is no way I can catch him. The match is over.

A new group greets us as we enter the clubhouse. They're mostly locals signing in for the twilight tournament. By now, George is introducing me as the best athlete ever to play at Amherst. Nobody can believe that he was able to beat me. The Bishop, as always, is gracious in victory. "I was lucky," he says. "Except for a fortunate bounce here and there, the match could have gone either way." Everyone looks at me knowingly.

I take it all in stride. Next year, it'll be a different story. Next year I'll be the winner, because next year I'm going to hire Little Ed as my caddie. Little Ed's just what I need to beat the Bishop.

‖ BALDFACE

I have a good friend from Mobile named Skipper Tonsmeire. I first met Skipper in 1975 when I was in charge of land acquisition for The Nature Conservancy. Even though he makes his living as a developer, Skipper spends most of his time working on conservation. It was Skipper who started the Conservancy's program in Alabama and expanded our conservation efforts across the Gulf Coast. Thanks to Skipper, the Conservancy was able to protect more than a half million acres of prime bottomland hardwood forests along the rivers of the Deep South.

Skipper has never been comfortable with me as a conservationist. He feels I'm too wedded to hot showers and soft beds to fully appreciate nature. When I visit him in Mobile, he makes me sleep on the floor of his fish camp and go swimming in the creek before breakfast. As I stand on his dock shivering, trying to find the nerve to jump in, he tells me, "Boy, get your Yankee butt in there. It'll get your blood moving, not to mention your spirit."

At least once a year, Skipper tries to lure me into the wilderness. I usually claim I'm too busy, but every now and then I get caught. Once he made me float the Tatshenshini River in Alaska. That's where I discovered the real Mother Nature. Conservationists like to portray Mother Nature as a young, anorexic waif who needs our protection. In reality, she's a mean old bitch who delights in floods, fires, hurricanes, and other natural disasters.

The real Mother Nature introduced herself to me when the Tatshenshini suddenly braided and my little raft went one way and Skipper's another. It was nine hours, a freezing rain, two raging rapids, and one big bear before the Tatshenshini came back together again. I'd been alone with Mother Nature the entire time. Skipper was delighted that I'd had such a unique wilderness experience. I was thankful to be alive. I never wanted to meet the real Mother Nature again.

The following year, Skipper proposed we go on a three-day hike over the Continental Divide followed by a four-day raft trip down the Salmon River. Instead, I suggested we spend a weekend at my cabin on Kezar. "You'll love Maine," I told him. "We can climb Baldface one day and canoe the Saco the next. Baldface is the best hike in the White Mountains, and the Saco's every bit as pretty as the Salmon. Why go to Idaho when Maine's got it all?" What I failed to mention is that my cabin has soft bunks, a hot shower, and no room for the real Mother Nature.

Skipper agreed to meet me at the Portland Jetport on October 1. When I arrived, he was there, but he wasn't alone. He was talking to an extremely attractive young woman dressed in tight Spandex slacks and a skimpy see-through blouse. "This is Lois," Skipper said, introducing me. "She's from L.A. Let's go." He picked up Lois's Gucci bag. Apparently, she was coming with us. I wasn't surprised. In his own quiet way, Skipper's something of a Lothario.

On the ride to Lovell, Lois told me that she'd met Skipper on the plane. His seat had been next to hers. Lois had never been to Maine and wanted to see the fall foliage. She'd planned to rent a car at the jetport and drive down east along the coast. During the flight, Skipper convinced her that the foliage would be much better in the mountains and invited her to come with us. Skipper could be quite persuasive.

When we arrived at the cabin, the sun was just setting. The mountains were aglow with fiery fall colors. Lois was immediately taken by the brilliant golds and reds. "Ohh," she gushed, "there's nothing like this in L.A."

"There's nothing like this anywhere," I told her. To prove my point, twelve loons came swimming out of the twilight. They dove in unison just before they reached the dock. "Fall's the only time you'll see that many together," I said, pleased that we were being treated to such a show. "This is when they raft up to head south."

With the sun down, a chill swept over the lake. Lois began to shiver. "I'll build us a fire," Skipper said. "Then we can get some steaks and cook 'em up."

"We'll do that tomorrow. I made reservations at the Center Lovell Inn for tonight. That's the place they sold by holding a raffle," I explained to Lois. "It was in all the papers. You might have read about it. In fact, the movie *The Spitfire Grill* is based on the Lovell Inn." I figured that, being from L.A., Lois would be impressed by the movie.

"Does it have heat?" she asked.

Richard and Janice Cox, the couple who'd won the raffle, did an excellent job. We had a wonderful meal, and Lois seemed genuinely glad that she'd joined us, at least until we got back to the cabin. It was freezing. Skipper built a roaring fire while I crawled into my soft, warm bunk. "I'm sleeping here next to the fire," I said, leaving the other bunk up for grabs.

"I'm sleeping on the porch," Skipper said, then added to Lois,

"You might want to try it out there. It'll get you close to nature."

I woke up to the sound of a crackling fire. Skipper was standing in front of the fireplace dressed in his sneakers, shorts, and a turtleneck. The turtleneck was stained with sweat. He'd already been for his morning run. "Get up, boy," he said, shaking the end of my sleeping bag. "It's time for a swim."

I looked out the window. The lake was covered with a dense mist. "Are you kidding?" I said. "This isn't Alabama. Nobody in Maine goes swimming in October. That water's freezing."

"The water's warmer than the air," Skipper said. "What do ya think's causing that mist?"

Skipper had a point. Skipper always had a point. Reluctantly, I climbed out of my nice warm sleeping bag and put on a swimsuit. As we went out, I saw a lump curled up in a sleeping bag on the cot in the corner of the porch. There was no sign of a head. Skipper gave the lump a pat. "Let's go, girl," he said. "Time for a swim." Nothing moved. I hoped Lois hadn't frozen during the night. We were a long way from L.A.

Gingerly, I stuck my toe in the water to test the temperature. Quickly, I pulled it out as a numbing cold rushed up my leg. Mist or no mist, there was no way that water was warmer than the air. "Whoa," I said. "This is not a good idea."

Skipper didn't hesitate. He waded in up to his waist, then dove like a loon. In the mist, I never saw him come up, but I could hear his steady stroke moving across the lake. "Come on, boy," he shouted from somewhere in the fog. Slowly, I walked out until the water was up to my waist. I stood there for a good ten minutes, letting my body acclimate. Surprisingly, the water started to feel pretty good.

The mist began to lift as the sun warmed the air. Patches of red and orange started to appear on the opposite shore. They were followed by bands of green as the mist burned off the hills. Soon, I was able to see the outline of the mountains. The last wisps of mist evaporated, exposing a cobalt blue sky, the kind you see from planes at 30,000 feet. Across the lake, Skipper was sunning himself on a rock. The bright fall sun was beginning to warm me up. I sucked in my gut, tensed my muscles, and took the plunge.

It was the best swim I'd ever had. The water temperature, the air temperature, the sun, the sky, the leaves, the trees, the hills, the mountains were all perfect. I was floating on my back, looking up at the mountains, when Skipper swam by. "Come on, boy," he said, "we've got things to do." Reluctantly, I followed him in. I never figured that I'd be swimming in Kezar Lake in October, but now that I was in, I didn't want to get out.

A hot shower had thawed Lois out, and after a big breakfast she insisted that we take her on a canoe ride around the lake so she could see the foliage. It was well after noon when we got back to the cabin. "Y'all ready to climb Baldface?" Skipper said.

The Baldface Range consists of two mountains, North and South Baldface. I had planned to take Skipper on the Circle Trail. According to the *Appalachian Mountain Club Guide*, "The Circle Trail makes a loop over North and South Baldface. It is one of the most attractive trips in the White Mountains, with about 4 mi. of open ledge with unobstructed views." The Circle Trail was 9.6 miles. The Appalachian Mountain Club's recommended time for completing the loop was six and a half hours, which meant it was too late for us to start climbing the Baldface Range.

There was an alternative: we could climb just one of the peaks. South Baldface was 7.2 miles with a recommended time of five hours. We'd have to move right along, but the sun was hot and there wasn't a cloud in the sky, so I said, "I guess we could do South Baldface."

I put on my sneakers, a pair of shorts, and a T-shirt. Even though it was October, it felt like summer. Lois was equally casual. She changed into a Calvin Klein aerobics outfit with a pair of designer sneakers and no socks. She looked like she'd stepped out of a fashion magazine. Skipper was the only one who dressed seriously. He wore a pair of Montrail TRS Comp II trail-running/speed-hiking shoes, Merino wool socks, Umbro shorts, and a Capiline zip turtleneck. He also carried a fanny pack. In it were matches, a knife, a bottle of water, a wool hat, and a Patagonia 60/40 High-Performance Guide Shell, the fundamental mountain parka.

We pulled into the AMC parking lot on Route 113 in Evans Notch just before two. The initial .7 mile was nothing more than a walk in the woods. Even though Skipper set a fast pace, Lois and I had no trouble keeping up. When we came to the split in the trail where one branch went to South Baldface and the other to North Baldface, I told Skipper, "Come down this path for a minute. I want to show you the Emerald Pool."

The pool is formed by Charles Brook, the drainage between North and South Baldface. It's naturally carved out of solid granite and has taken on the color of the dark green moss that clings to the rock. The water is so clear that the pool only looks a few feet deep. Actually, it's twelve. Most people climb down to get in. Experienced hikers jump from the top.

"Y'all want to take a swim?" Skipper said. It was still pretty hot and we were sweating.

"No, not now," I said. "We'll jump in on our way back. A dip in the Emerald Pool is the reward for climbing Baldface."

For the next 1.8 miles, the trail wound though deciduous forest up the east side of South Baldface. Lois slipped once or twice on loose rocks, but other than that she had no trouble. At 2.5 miles, the trail swung to the left, and we came to Last Chance Spring and the AMC shelter. From this point, South Baldface is arguably the best climb in the White Mountains. In 1903, the top third of the mountain was swept by fire. The forest has never grown back, so there's nothing but open views from here to the summit.

This point also marks the start of the ledges, a series of granite outcroppings that run for .5 mile and are by far the most difficult part of the hike. Scaling the ledges is like climbing up a steep roof. On dry summer days it's fun, but a storm must have come through the night before, because that day the rocks were wet. I'd never climbed the ledges when they were wet. I was surprised, but not hurt, when I slipped and fell on the first ledge, a huge, flat rock with almost no pitch. "Watch yourself," I said to Lois. "These rocks are like ice."

Lois wasn't taking any chances. She got down on her hands and knees and began to crawl. It wasn't a bad idea. I did the same. Skipper's Montrail TRS Comp II trail-running/speed-hiking shoes gave him some traction, but it was still slow going. "Just a little farther," I kept telling Lois. "I see the top of the ledges. Once we get there, it's a piece of cake."

Lois was tougher than she looked. She kept climbing on her hands and knees. By the time we reached the top, the knees of her Calvin Klein outfit were gone, but she hadn't complained once. As we stopped to catch our breath, I noticed that the weather was deteriorating. The cobalt blue sky was now slate gray, but it was still warm out, at least until I stuck my head up over the last ledge. There I was greeted by a blast of arctic air. Mount Washington, the site of the highest winds ever recorded in North America, stood directly in front of us. Its top was engulfed in swirling snow. The mercury was falling out of the thermometer. The real Mother Nature was saying hello.

"I don't like the looks of that," Skipper said. "Let's go back." He turned and started down the ledges.

"I'm not going down those rocks," Lois said. She sat down and folded her arms, refusing to move. I couldn't blame her.

Going up the ledges was a lot easier than going down. I wasn't eager to tackle them in my sneakers.

"What do ya want to do?" Skipper asked me.

I looked up at the summit of South Baldface, then over to the summit of North Baldface. They were both clear, at least for the time being. "We could take the Circle Trail," I said. "I've never done it, but it has to be easier than going back down the ledges."

Skipper took off his fanny pack and pulled out three granola bars. "Eat this," he said, giving us each a bar. Next he took out the wool hat and the Patagonia parka. "Put these on," he said, tossing them to Lois. Then he turned and started following the cairns up the trail.

A half hour and .6 mile later, we reached the summit of South Baldface, elevation 3,569 feet. We didn't stop to admire the view. The storm had worked its way across Pinkham Notch. Mount Washington was gone. The first flakes of snow started swirling around us. The sweat I'd broken on the way up was freezing to my cotton T-shirt, turning it into a cooler.

The AMC's recommended time to traverse the 1.1-mile ridge between the two summits is forty minutes. Despite two steep, rocky ascents, we did it in thirty. The snow was steady and starting to accumulate by the time we reached the summit of North Baldface, elevation 3,591 feet. I wasn't sure what Mother Nature had in store for us over the next 4.9 miles, but I knew it wasn't going to be good. The snow was making the trail very slippery, and the lack of foliage was leaving us totally exposed. I'd read stories about people who'd gotten caught by storms up in the Presidentials, but I never thought I'd be one of them. I could look down on the Lower Bay. Seeing it now through the snow, it was hard to imagine we'd gone swimming that morning.

The trail down from the summit of North Baldface was not as bad as the ledges, but it wasn't good. There were numerous spots where Skipper and I had to stop and help Lois over the rocks. We were making lousy time, and now, in addition to dealing with the snow, we were losing daylight. After about a mile, we came to two AMC signs pointing in opposite directions. One read "N. Baldface" and pointed back toward the summit; the other, "Eagle Link Trail," continued along the spine of the ridge we'd been following. There was nothing about the Circle Trail. "This ain't right," Skipper said.

There was a series of cairns leading down into the bowl formed by the two Baldfaces, but were they the Circle Trail? Given my casual approach to hiking, I'd neglected to bring my AMC map. I cleaned snow from my glasses. "This has to be the Circle Trail," I said, pointing at the cairns. "If it isn't, it has to meet up with it sooner or later."

"Let's take it," Skipper said. "We gotta get out of this snow."

No sooner had we gone a hundred yards than we encountered a steep ledge. At the bottom, we could see the woods. There was no snow in them. "Get between us," Skipper said to Lois. "We're going down."

Skipper helped Lois from the front while I did what I could from the back. She spent most of the time sliding down the ledge on her butt. By the time we reached the woods, the seat of her Calvin Klein pants was as bare as the knees. Lois no longer looked like she'd stepped out of a fashion magazine. She looked like a refugee.

For the next two hours we picked our way down the mountain. We were out of the snow, but at times we had trouble finding the trail. Near the bottom, we came to an intersection. It turned out that we'd been on the Bicknell Ridge Trail, which, according to the AMC guidebook, is "a scenic route to the valley" and a longer, more difficult trail. The Circle Trail had been farther along the ridge. We'd missed it by a quarter of a mile.

The night was cold, dark, and rainy by the time we stumbled past the Emerald Pool. My legs felt like rubber; my feet were frozen. "Y'all gonna take that swim?" Skipper said.

Lois and I never broke stride. We'd completed the loop in less than six hours, which, given the conditions and the fact that we'd missed the trail intersection, was quite an accomplishment. One thing was sure: Never again would I take hiking in the mountains casually. Even on the nicest of days, I'd wear boots instead of sneakers and carry a pack with extra clothes, water, a knife, matches, a compass, and maps. We'd been lucky, and I knew it. You don't mess around with the real Mother Nature.

HAVE A
WONDERFUL WEEK

Anyone lucky enough to have a place in Vacationland has been asked at one time or another, "If you're not using your place, would you mind if we borrowed it for a few days?"

This question is most often posed by close friends or family members, and while you'd like to tell them, "Mind? You bet we mind. Our cabin is very special, and having you or anybody else there without us is unthinkable," what you actually say is, "Er, um, well, er, I guess that would be okay."

As soon as the words leave your lips, you get a sinking feeling in your stomach. What have you done? How can you condone the unsupervised invasion of your special place? The thought of pumps, generators, firewood, docks, boats, screens, and shutters flutter through your mind. Each has its own idiosyncrasies; each must be babied and coddled with kid gloves. Don't they realize that maintaining a cabin requires the brains of Thomas Edison, the brawn of Paul Bunyan, and the ingenuity of Rube Goldberg? Mastering all of its intricacies takes the better part of a lifetime.

You start making a list of the dos and don'ts. Over the years, I've prepared dozens of these lists. Each is custom-tailored to the brains, brawn, and ingenuity of our guests, but they all have one thing in common: They're all exceedingly polite and never say what I really mean. Although I want to lay down the law, my law, I inevitably end up with cheery notes suggesting how things might go better if our guests were to do this or that. The lists inevitably start with the phoney greeting, "Welcome. We're glad you'll be using the cabin for a few days. Here are a few tips to make your stay more enjoyable."

What I really want to say is: We can't believe you had the nerve to turn your "few days" into a full week with two weekends, but now that you've weaseled your way into the best part of the summer, we hope you won't screw anything up. Here's how we do things around here. These aren't tips; they're your Bible. There will be absolutely no deviations.

Then I move on to specifics.

- Septic. Our septic system is subject to constipation at the slightest irritation. The less you flush, the better it will be. "If it's yellow, let it mellow. If it's brown, flush it down." PLEASE do not put any foreign objects in the bowl.

What I mean is: Thanks to a whole bunch of new environmental regulations, we had to install a very expensive but very sensitive septic system. DON'T SCREW IT UP! Keep pads, tampons, and all other junk out of the bowl. This isn't like home where you have city sewerage. Mess up, and you'll be in deep shit.

- Trash. Attached are the latest regulations from the dump. As you can see, Maine is heavily into recycling. NOTE: The dump is only open on certain days. Time your departure accordingly. Please

don't leave any trash in the cabin. It draws
animals.

What I mean is: Thanks to the lobbying efforts of all the do-gooders in the environmental movement (my colleagues), everything has to be recycled. All this recycling is a pain. We spend half our vacation buried up to our elbows sorting cans, papers, clear glass, colored glass, plastics, and biodegradable garbage. Make sure you go to the dump before you leave. The last thing we want to do is have to sort through your garbage!

- Fires. If you use the fireplace, be sure to open the damper. Firewood is under the porch. So is the maul. As the old New England saying goes, "Split your own wood and it warms you twice."

What I mean is: Aged, dry firewood is a precious commodity. We've laid in a supply for the season and don't want to go through the hassle of cutting more. If you want a fire, split your own damn wood. If you get cold and don't want to do that, wrap yourself in a blanket and have another snort.

- Boats. Please feel free to use the canoe. Cushions, paddles, and life jackets are under the porch. Please do not use the motorboat or the sailboat. We didn't register them this year, and if you get caught using them, you'll be fined. Rental boats are available at the marina.

What I mean is: I lied. Sailboats and motors under five horse-power don't have to be registered. We just don't want you using them. There are lots of rocks in the cove, and unless you know what you're doing, which you don't, you're going to pile into them. The canoe is the most maneuverable, but don't bang it up.

What we'd really like you to do is go down to the marina and rent your own boat.

- The Dock. Be careful; it's not too steady and it gets very slippery when wet.

What I mean is: I designed and built the dock myself. That's why it's so unsteady. If you don't know exactly where to walk, you could slip and fall on your head. The last thing I need is you suing me. I just pray you're covered under my homeowner's policy. If I had the nerve, I'd ask you to sign a waiver. But I don't, so don't get hurt.

- Pets. If you bring a pet, please keep it tied up on the porch and don't let it bother the wildlife.

What I mean is: Pets are a nuisance. They track in dirt and sand, shed hair on the furniture, scratch the wood floors, rip the screens, crap on the beach, harass the wildlife, and annoy the neighbors. I have to put up with our pets but not yours, so leave them at home or put them in a kennel.

- Wildlife. Respect all birds and animals, and please don't get too close to the loons. As the Pequaw-kets, the aboriginal inhabitants of the Saco River Valley, used to say, we are the guests.

What I mean is: Don't bother the wildlife. Don't let your kids catch frogs down by the beach, and don't kill the occasional water snake or snapping turtle that comes by. They won't bother you if you don't bother them. If you want to get a good look at the loons, use binoculars. And *do not* feed the chipmunks and squirrels. If you think they're cute now, try having them in your place for the winter. Living close to nature is a big part of being in Maine, but don't disturb it.

- Rodney. If you have a problem, call Rodney. Rodney built the cabin and knows everything about
  it. He probably can tell you what's wrong over the
  phone. His number, along with other emergency
  numbers, is on the wall.

What I mean is: If anything goes wrong, call Rodney, but don't just ask him to come over. Get him to tell you over the phone how to fix whatever's wrong. If Rodney comes over, we have to pay him, and that gets expensive. Hopefully, you can figure out what has to be done, but knowing you, I doubt it.

My conclusion usually goes something like this:

- That's about it. Please leave the cabin as you
  found it, and if you have any questions, feel free
  to give us a call. We're delighted that you're able
  to use our place, and have a wonderful week!

What I mean is: I could add a million more things to this list, but what's the use? You probably won't read it anyway. We really hope you don't move things around. Our cabin is like a boat; there's a place for everything and everything's in its place. And please don't call us. We don't want to hear about any problems, and we know you're having a wonderful week. How could anybody at our cabin not have a wonderful week? We're just frustrated that we can't be there ourselves. Enjoy it while you can. Next year, we plan to be in Maine for THE ENTIRE SUMMER.

If only that were the end of it. But it isn't. Inevitably, guests feel that they have to leave us a gift, something they think will enhance the cabin. They can't seem to understand that we have everything just the way we want it. In addition to countless mugs, pillows, mats, stuffed dolls, and assorted knickknacks with pictures of loons and moose on them, some of the more useless gifts we've received are:

An electric grill.

This guest knew that I loved to cook out down by the beach, so he bought me an electric grill and a long, heavy-duty orange extension cord so I could set up the grill on the very rocks I use to build my campfire. What he failed to understand is that the romance lies in cooking over an open fire.

An indoor/outdoor thermometer

This one really cracked me up, since the temperature is always the same inside and out. The guests who gave us the thermometer came in fall, so I think they were trying to send us a message. Namely, Get some heat!

Wind chimes

I hate those things. I come to Maine to hear the wind whistling through the pines, not some artificial tinkling. Wind chimes are fine in the city where they can block out street noise, but they have no place in Maine. In Maine, the sounds should be natural.

A bug zapper

There is great satisfaction in seeing your enemies zapped, but the blue glow and the constant *bzzzzts* were more annoying than the bugs. Plus, a lot of innocent moths are "drawn to the flame." The zapper had to go.

The best gift we ever got was by accident. Our friends Bobby and Cheryl Harrington forgot to pack their griddle after they stayed at the cabin for a weekend. It was one of those cast-iron jobs that set atop the burners. Ruth loved it. She was making pancakes, eggs, bacon, and French toast when Cheryl called to ask for it back. When Ruth raved about it and wondered where we could get one, Cheryl said, "Keep it. That'll be our gift to the cabin." The Harringtons are always welcome at our place in Maine.

What I actually say and what I'd like to say will never be the same. Despite my grumblings, I know that if you're lucky enough to have a place in Maine, you can't begrudge your close friends and relatives a few days in paradise. They'll all do their best to keep it nice, and most will love it as much as you do. So when close friends and relatives ask if they can borrow your cabin, it doesn't do any good to get all huffy and start making lists. The best approach is to smile, give them the key, and say, "HAVE A WONDERFUL WEEK!"

DONNA'S DOMAINE

One guest who knew Mom well left us an unusually thoughtful gift. She wrote a poem about Mom. It told how Mom loved Kezar, how she finally found her lot, how she liked to sit on her rock and look into the mountains, how she dreamed of building her "dollhouse," and how her spirit will always be with us whenever we're in Maine. The poem was called "Donna's Domaine." We framed it and hung it on the wall, and from then on the cabin was known as Donna's Domaine.

Although "Donna's Domaine" lacks the mystique of names like Little Beaver or Arrowhead or Loon's Nest, it's appropriate because Mom's spirit does dominate our life in Maine. The antiques shops she frequented, the homes she could have bought, and the churches she attended are all constant reminders. It's tough to go anywhere in the Saco River Valley without thinking about her, but Mom's spirit used to be especially strong at the Lovell United Church of Christ. That was her favorite.

I'm not a religious person, at least in the traditional sense of the word. I was brought up an Episcopalian, but as a kid I hated going to church. The service was too long and too boring. The hymns were the only thing I enjoyed. When I was old enough to start making my own decisions, I stopped going to church. It's a decision I've regretted only once.

In the fall of 1975, I was in Boston for a conference. The meeting ended Saturday afternoon, and rather than fly back to Washington, I decided to visit my parents. It was good I did. I knew Mom had cancer, but I didn't know she was going into the hospital the next day. That evening, Dad and Mom and I went out to dinner and had an enjoyable time. The next morning, I was lying in bed listening to Mom get ready for church. I thought about going with her, but changed my mind. The prospect of having to sit through another long, boring service was too much for me. I stayed home to visit with Dad.

That afternoon, Dad and I dropped Mom off at Massachusetts General Hospital. After we'd gotten her checked in, Dad took me to the airport. As I was getting out of the car, I noticed a program from the church on the back seat. There was a picture of Mom on the cover. Inside were more pictures of Mom handing Bibles to Africans and Asians. Next to the pictures were testimonials from religious leaders all over the world. This was a big deal. While I was lying in bed, St. John's Episcopal Church in Arlington, Massachusetts, had been honoring Mom for the forty years she'd dedicated to "Bibles for the World." Mom had never said a word about it. On one of the most important days of her life, none of her boys had been with her. And that was bad. She died two weeks later.

While we were building the cabin, Ruth saw that the Right Reverend George L. Cadigan was going to be the guest preacher at the Lovell United Church of Christ. Given our friendship with George, we decided to go. It was the most enjoyable service I'd ever been to. Every pew was filled, we knew a lot of people, and the hymns were all old favorites. Plus, the Bishop's sermon was outstanding. He talked about how Kezar was our spiritual home and confessed that whenever he was stuck in a dull ecclesiastical meeting, he'd imagine being in a canoe moving quietly up Sucker Brook. "Suddenly and awesomely I'm transported into another world," he said, "a world you and I love very much."

As the Bishop described paddling up Sucker Brook, the congregation was suddenly and awesomely transported into another world—a world we loved very much. I could picture the morning mist over the water; the long, loping flight of a great blue heron; the trilling of a red-winged blackbird; the hesitant motions of a deer in the shallows; the splash of a turtle; the rise of a fish; the brilliant red of the cardinal flowers. When the Bishop concluded by saying, "and we were at one with ourselves and with all of creation," I knew exactly what he meant.

Ruth and I liked everything about the Lovell United Church of Christ. I could see why it was Mom's favorite. All through the service, I felt her presence. After that, whenever we were in Maine, we went to church. Don Morrison, the regular minister, was no Bishop Cadigan, but he was honest and sincere and ran a good service. Don was a few years younger than I, sported a big handlebar mustache, and was prone to malapropisms. My favorite was the time he confused testaments with tenements. I could picture the apostles in strappy T-shirts, leaning out third-story windows of run-down apartment buildings, hanging up the laundry and extolling the covenant between man and God.

Once a summer, Don would have Hymn Sunday. Instead of a sermon, members of the congregation would shout out the number of their favorite hymn. Hearing a number, Mary Wilson, the organist, would launch into the first verse. Mary Wilson knew every hymn, and the congregation of Lovell United knew every word. The singing was loud, spirited, and full of good cheer.

For two years, the church was an enjoyable part of our time in Maine. Then, one winter, we heard that Don had been fired. Word had it that the vestry had become upset because he'd taken a night job as a bartender at the Pleasant Mountain ski area. I could see Don behind a bar. He showed up at softball every now and then and mixed easily with even the most lost members of Lovell's flock. He was a regular guy who could minister outside the church. "Judge not, lest ye be judged."

Don's firing split the church and the community. We went to one service the next summer, but the Lovell United Church of Christ was no longer united. The pews were half empty. The minister was some circuit rider with a canned sermon. The singing was barely audible, half-hearted, and dour. Mom's presence was gone, and we never went back. Instead, on Sunday mornings Ruth and I would get in the *Ruda* and paddle up Sucker Brook.

One Sunday morning, I was getting ready to launch the *Ruda* when a huge water snake suddenly appeared. I'm not a big fan of snakes, especially water snakes. I don't like to go swimming if I know that something that big is slinking around. I grabbed a rock and was about to throw it at the snake when a memory from Jordan's Camps seized my arm.

At Jordan's, we used to have our own special version of cowboys and Indians, one with a local twist. Lovewell Pond was named for Captain John Lovewell, a member of the Massachusetts militia from Dunstable. On the morning of May 8, 1725, Captain Lovewell and his company of thirty-four rangers came across a party of eighty Pequawket Indians camped on the northwest corner of the lake. The Pequawkets were led by Paugus, a respected warrior and able chief. The Pequawkets, like most other tribes in the North, were allies of the French, but due to a lull in the French and Indian Wars, Paugus and his braves were not expecting any trouble. They were enjoying the day fishing and resting by the shore, out of the woods and away from the blackflies.

War or no war, the Commonwealth of Massachusetts wanted to get rid of all the Indians in its northern territory and was offering a bounty of fifty cents for any Indian's scalp. Lovewell and his company of thirty-four rangers were traipsing through the Saco River Valley looking for bounty. Finding Paugus and his eighty braves basking on the shore of this unnamed lake was a financial bonanza. A quick massacre could net Lovewell and his company forty bucks. That was sixteen more dollars than Dutchman Peter Minuit had paid for Manhattan Island exactly one hundred years earlier.

There was only one problem. Lovewell and his thirty-four rangers had discovered Paugus and his braves on a Sunday morning, and the captain didn't think it would be Christian to conduct a massacre on the Sabbath. In need of spiritual guidance, Lovewell consulted the company's chaplain, Jonathan Frye, from Andover. Young Frye was engaged to be married that June and had come on the expedition to make some money. Frye advised Lovewell that letting these heathen scalps get away would be sinful, not to mention bad business. He urged the captain to attack immediately.

Paugus and his braves were no pushovers. The battle raged from morning until sunset, when what remained of the Pequawkets finally staggered to their birch-bark canoes and retreated down the Saco River. According to a monument erected on the site in 1904 by the Massachusetts Society of Colonial Wars, Lovewell and thirteen of his men were killed on the field, as was Paugus. Frye was critically wounded and died on the way home to his fiancée in Andover. There is no mention on the monument of how many scalps were taken, but the lake was named for Lovewell, and Frye got the "burg."

All the kids at Jordan's would row across the pond once a

summer to visit the monument and read about the battle. When we got back to camp, we'd choose up sides and have our own fight. The older kids were the rangers, the younger, the Pequaw-kets. Not that it made much difference. Either way, most of us ended up lying facedown in the sand.

Our battle at Jordan's in '52 had been raging for most of the morning. We were having a wonderful time throwing rubber tomahawks and shooting off rolls of caps we'd bought at Solari's. I was a husky little brave. Bobby Garland, Richard Cunningham, and Ted, each of whom fancied himself as Captain Lovewell, were the rangers. When they discovered me hiding between some boats on the beach, a volley of caps finished me off before I could raise my tomahawk. I rolled over in the sand, dead.

I didn't stay dead very long. When I opened my eyes, a big water snake was staring right at me. Its head couldn't have been a yard from my face. I hollered and jumped to my feet. Bobby Garland, Richard Cunningham, and Ted let loose with another volley of caps aimed at me, then, seeing the snake, holstered their guns and let loose with a volley of rocks aimed at the snake. The snake, unlike Paugus and his braves, put up no fight. It immediately retreated, its body whipping back and forth like a bolt of lightning. I'd never seen anything that big swim that fast.

This should have been the end of it, but it wasn't. Mr. Cunningham had heard me hollering and came running down to the beach. "What happened, Davey?" the Deacon asked. Before I could answer, Ted took charge. "A huge snake just attacked Davey," he said. "And there it is!" Ted pointed to the lake. Sure enough, about fifty feet out, the snake's head was gliding slowly through the water. The swim must have tired it out; it was heading for shore. We all watched as it came out of the water and slithered up on the rocks a couple of hundred yards down the beach.

"Let's kill it," Bobby Garland said.

We all looked to the Deacon for guidance. What the Deacon should have said was, "Leave it alone; it's not hurting anybody," but he didn't. Like Chaplain Frye, the Deacon showed no mercy. "Bobby's right," he said. "Let's kill it."

We all threw down our cap guns and rubber tomahawks, picked up sticks and stones, and charged down the beach. We cornered the snake on the rocks and began peppering it with everything we had. When the snake tried to squiggle back into the water, the Deacon pinned it with an oar. "Get a rock and hit it on the head," the Deacon commanded. While the rest of us froze, Bobby Garland grabbed a big stone and dropped it squarely on the snake's head. That was it; the snake was a goner.

The Deacon hoisted it over the oar and marched proudly back to camp. He placed the snake on a tree stump just up from the beach. With our Eden saved, the Deacon went back to his camp. We stood around the stump studying our handiwork. It wasn't a pleasant sight. Somehow the snake was still alive, but just barely. Its tongue kept flicking in and out of its crushed head. That's when Mr. Largess came by. We all were convinced that Mr. Largess was part Indian. He wore real moccasins, carved little totem poles, and knew all about nature.

"What the hell have you kids done?" he said, looking at the snake. We all looked at our feet. "What in God's good name did this snake ever do to you to deserve this?"

It was a good question, but the Deacon wasn't there to answer it. Nobody said a word; none of us dared look up. Mr. Largess shook his head in disgust and gently picked up the snake. He tried to balance it over both arms, but it was too big. "You kids get the hell out of here," he said.

We'd never seen Mr. Largess mad. Nobody was ever mad at Jordan's. He took the snake up in the woods and didn't come back for a long time. I felt guilty and ashamed. It was the worst moment I'd ever had at Jordan's Camps. That experience didn't make me like snakes any better, but I never forgot it. It was that memory which kept me from throwing a rock at another snake on a Sunday morning at kezar lake, so many years later.

This snake was just moseying along the shore, I assumed looking for frogs. I expected it to keep moving, but it didn't. When it came to Mom's rock, it stopped. "Damn," I said to Ruth, who'd come down for our Sunday morning canoe ride up Sucker Brook. "Will you look at that. A water snake's crawling up on Mom's rock."

"It's very beautiful," Ruth said. Ruth's something of a mini Medusa; she likes snakes.

"Well, it can be beautiful someplace else. I don't want any snakes hanging around here."

I got a stick and gently prodded the snake on its way. I was hoping we'd never see it again, but a strange thing has happened. It, or a snake just like it, keeps showing up at least once a year. It always curls up on Mom's rock, its head looking towards the mountains. When it's there, I feel Mom's presence, the same as I did at the Lovell United Church of Christ.

Kezar Lake is my spiritual home, and being at one with nature is my religion. Still, I refuse to take a swim with the snake sitting there. As the sun gets hotter and the water becomes more and more inviting, I take a stick and gently prod the reptile on its way. That upsets Ruth. "Why do you do that?" she asks. "It's not bothering anybody."

"It's bothering me," I say. "Church is over. It's time for me to take a swim and for this snake to be on its way."

I'm sure Mom wouldn't mind. When we were in Maine, she never stayed in camp very long. Mom liked moving around. That's why her spirit dominates Donna's Domaine.

HOME FREE!

"It's Thursday," Ruth said. "Why don't you go up to Westways and play softball?"

"I beg your pardon," I said, putting my book down.

"I'm going to the concert at the church tonight," she said. "I know you don't want to do that, so why don't you go play softball? It'll do you good to get out."

It had been raining all week, and Ruth and I were developing a slight case of cabin fever. That's why she was going to the concert and undoubtedly why she suggested Thursday night softball for me. I looked at the lake. Sunbeams were dancing on the water. It had been getting lighter all day, and the late-afternoon sun had finally broken through. It was going to be a nice evening, but I hadn't played Thursday night softball since I'd collided with Paul McLaughlin, Tom and Dan McLaughlin's six-foot-two, 250-pound baby brother. That had been five years earlier.

"I'm too old to play softball," I said. "I've got bursitis in my shoulder, so I can't throw, and with these damn bifocals, I doubt I can hit."

"Plus, you don't hear very well," Ruth added gratuitously.

"My hearing's got nothing to do with it," I said, "but I can't go up there. I haven't played in five years. Most of the old guys are probably gone and I don't know any of the new kids."

"With all this rain, they might need an extra man," Ruth persisted. "And if you don't like it, you don't have to stay. Just come home."

Ruth knew how much I loved Thursday night softball at Westways. All through the eighties, it had been one of my greatest joys. I used to plan my whole summer schedule so I could be in Lovell on Thursday nights. I could feel the old juices starting to stir. It would be good to get out, and Ruth was right: if I didn't like it, I didn't have to stay. I rocked up from my chair, pulled my Playmate cooler out from under the porch, packed a six-pack of Sam Adams, dug out my glove, boxed my hat, and strapped on my bifocals. I was ready to play ball.

"Okay," I said to Ruth, "I'll drop by and see what's happening. If some of the old guys are still there, I might stick around for a couple of innings."

I pulled in next to a row of battered pickups and marveled at the green of the grass, the blue of the lake, and the purple of the mountains. I'd forgotten how special this little diamond at Westways was, how it glowed in the evening light, how it nestled among the towering pines. The sound of softballs slapping against leather and the ping of a metal bat said that it was Thursday night. I grabbed my Playmate, straightened my hat, spit in my glove, and headed for the field. I was back.

Ruth was right. Normally, there'd be fifteen to twenty guys warming up. Tonight, there were barely a dozen, most of them familiar faces. John Bliss, the local surveyor, was busy laying out the bases. Tom McLaughlin, the former first selectman, was playing catch with Eddy Nista, the current chairman of the board of appeals. Angelo Campo, a computer jockey who still looked like a short, husky Fidel Castro, was hitting fungos to Bob Drew, the electrician who'd first introduced me to Thursday night softball.

Bob Aiken, the manager of the K-Mart over in North Con-way, was raking away the puddles around home plate with Mark Tripp, the caretaker at Westways. A ball went streaking over their heads and banged off the top of the backstop. Sure enough, there was Steven Bennett in deep center field loosening up his powerful but ever erratic arm. On the bench drinking a beer was Hopie, Lovell's oldest and best hippie. "Hey, look what the cat dragged in," Hopie said as I approached the bench.

"Well, with all this rain, I thought you guys might need an extra glove."

"Damn straight," Hopie said. "It takes a few innings for these new kids to show up. No dedication. Lousy values."

"Stephen King still come?" I said, trying to give myself some credibility.

"Naw, Steve's too old, but his kid plays every now and then." So much for my credibility.

When we got to sixteen, John Bliss and Eddie Nista quietly stepped aside to choose up the teams. I remembered when I used to fancy myself as a top pick. Now, I was just happy to be chosen at all.

"Dave, you're in the field," John Bliss said to me when they were done. "Where do you want to play?"

With only sixteen, there'd be no catcher. "I'll take right," I said. "That way, maybe I can stay out of trouble."

"Okay, but try not to run into anyone. Haw, haw."

My first at bat came at the bottom of the second. There were two outs and men on first and second. Steven Bennett was on the mound. Even with slow pitch, Steven was having trouble finding the strike zone. "Come on, Dave, there's two ducks on the pond," John Bliss said. "All we need is a little bingo."

I rummaged through the bat rack looking for the Ball Buster, my old wooden bat. During my absence, everyone had switched to metal bats, shiny black cannons made with space-age alloys, but I was a purist and believed that real bats were made of wood. Amazingly, the Ball Buster was still there, but I hardly recognized it. Its bright red gloss had been bleached white, and the lettering was barely discernible. We were a good match, this old bat and I, a couple of relics trying to recapture the past.

I took a few practice swings and stepped into the batter's box. Little bingo, my eye. I was going for the tennis court. I was going to reintroduce myself with a three-run blast. I went after the first pitch. It was just above the letters, but Steven Bennett wasn't any Hopie. I wasn't going to see any meatballs from him.

A decent ballplayer should have been able to reach up and get that pitch, but thanks to my bifocals, I reached too high and topped the ball. It dribbled toward third. I chugged toward first. Tom McLaughlin, who usually had a vacuum cleaner for a glove, slipped on the wet grass and bobbled the ball. There was no play at third or second, so he rifled a shot to first. Mark Tripp gave it one of his classic stretches, and even with Tom's bobble, I was out by a yard.

"Gee, Dave, looks like you've lost a step or two—or three or four," Hopie said as I hobbled back to the bench.

My next two at bats were equally disappointing. A little pop to short, followed by a soft liner to second, each with "ducks on the pond," each snuffing out a potential rally. Thanks in large part to my anemic performance, we were down by eight runs going into the bottom of the seventh. I was tempted to call it quits, especially when a couple of pickups pulled in and a bunch of young bucks piled out. Everyone who shows up for Thursday night softball plays, so they immediately worked their way into the lineup. The best ended up on our side, and their powerful bats quickly whittled away the eight-run lead. Steven Bennett shook his head in disgust as shot after shot sailed into the woods. Going into the bottom of the ninth, we were down by just one.

Like all good athletes, Steven and his side began to bear down. Our first batter sent a scorcher down the third-base line, but Tom McLaughlin looked like Brooks Robinson as he neatly backhanded the ball and fired to first. Our young buck was fast, but not fast enough. Mark Tripp gave another classic stretch, and Hopie, the catcher, called our guy out.

The next kid launched a rocket to center. It had extra bases written all over it, but one of their young bucks sprinted back and made a Willie Mays over-the-shoulder catch. It was unbelievable. As I popped my last Sam Adams, I was glad the game was almost over. These new kids were way out of my league.

Angelo waddled to the plate. He was our last chance. He gave his Fidel Castro beard a tug and cracked the first pitch deep, deep to left. The ball bounced off a big pine and rolled into the woods. It would have been a homer for almost anyone, but Angelo was lucky to make third. He fell on the bag huffing and puffing. Now the tying run was just sixty feet from the plate.

"Atta boy, Angie!" John Bliss shouted. "Who's up?"

One of our young bucks hopped to his feet, his muscles swelling under a Maine Coon T-shirt. "Must be me," he said.

"Whoa, wait a minute," Hopie said from behind the plate. "Dave's up."

A dejected look swept across our bench. Hopie was right. I was up. What a terrible way to end a great game. We'd almost come back. Fortunately, even the young guys were too polite to say anything. I chugged what was left of my beer, trudged over to the bat box, and pulled out the Ball Buster. For a brief moment, I thought of switching to metal but resisted the temptation. I took a couple of practice swings and stepped up to the plate.

"Hey, Dave," Hopie said from under his mask, "here's your big chance. Hit one into the woods and you'll be a hero." Hopie's voice dripped with sarcasm. Gone was the sincerity of the sixties.

I didn't say a thing. I was too busy looking for some hole in the defense. Dan McLaughlin, knowing my lack of power, had everyone playing in. Bob, the manager at K-Mart, was the only one out of position. Bob was playing right, and seeing that I was a righty, he was shading me too far to the left. My only hope was to try to punch one down the right-field line. To do that, I'd need an outside pitch. I'd have to hope that Steven Bennett put one out there.

Steven's powerful arm still couldn't find the plate. His first three offerings were high, low, and inside. With a 3–0 count, a new strategy emerged. I could go for a walk. No decent ballplayer ever walked at Thursday night softball. Anyone with three balls and anything less than two strikes automatically took a mock swing at ball four. Not me. Not anymore. I wasn't going to lose this game. I was too old to be humiliated. I'd take a free pass if Steven offered it.

"Come on, Steve," Hopie yelled from behind me. "Pitch to this guy. Make him hit."

Steve's next pitch came floating over the outside corner of the plate. It would have been a ball, but instinct took over. The old Ball Buster reached out and smacked it. It was a beautiful shot, perfect in every way, right over the first-base bag. Mark Tripp leaped into the air, but he didn't have enough spring. The ball zoomed six inches above his outstretched glove.

I raced to first, my old legs churning like a teenager's. I watched the ball bounce just inside of the big birch that marks the right-field line and dug deeper as it skipped into the woods.

Bob was running after it, and one of the young bucks was moving over to get the cutoff, but it was going to take them a while to catch up with that shot. Angelo was home. This game was tied and I was going for two, maybe more.

As I motored toward second, I could hear a chorus of rich Maine accents yelling from our bench. "Home free! Home free!" As I rounded second, the cry got louder. *"Home free! Home free!"* I couldn't believe it. They were telling me to go for home. I was going to score. I was going to win this friggin' game.

I could see the amazed look on Tom McLaughlin's face as I streaked around third. Base coaches are far too formal for Thursday night softball, but I didn't need a third-base coach. The cries I heard coming from the bench were now almost hysterical. "HOME FREE!! HOME FREE!!"

Hopie was standing at the plate. He discarded his mask and pounded his glove, obviously trying to deke me out. What did he think I was, some rookie? Couldn't he hear the screams? I was going "Home free!"

I was about twenty feet from the plate when Hopie casually caught the ball. There was no chance of stopping and trying to scramble back to third. I had too much momentum. I was like a supertanker heading for an iceberg. "Too bad," Hopie said as he tagged me out.

John Bliss caught me just before I collapsed. "Jeez, Dave," he said. "Why'd you keep running?"

"I heard you all yelling 'Home free! Home free!' I thought I had it," I gasped.

"'Home free?'" John said. "We were yelling 'Hold three. Hold three.' A triple would have been plenty from you."

That was it. The game was over. The sun had long set behind the Presidential Range. Evening shadows crept over the field. Nobody cared that the score was tied. A tie was fine for Thursday night softball.

"Not too bad for an old man," Hopie said as I was getting into my car. "Only next week, take the potatoes out of your ears."

I wasn't sure there'd be a next week. Already I could feel my body stiffening. I'd be sore all over in the morning. Still, it was worth it. Seeing that ball bounce into the woods, running the bases, hearing the cheers. I couldn't wait to get back and tell Ruth. I just wouldn't mention the part about "Home free."

VIVA LA MAINE

The Fourth of July has always been my favorite holiday. That's because I've spent most of my Fourths in Maine. When I was a kid, we'd have a cookout with red hot dogs on the beach at Jordan's, then when it got dark watch a Roman candle somebody'd set off across the lake. Sitting around the fire, roasting marshmallows, watching the distant candle spit rockets up into the Milky Way—that was about as good as it got.

After we built our cabin on Kezar, Ruth and I would drive up to Bethel for the Fourth. We'd meet Rodney and Carol on the town common, have a picnic supper, and listen to the concert. There was always at least one Jordan grandchild playing at the Bethel bandstand. After the concert, we'd walk across the street to the Bethel Inn and lie on the golf course to watch the fireworks. This small-town celebration couldn't hold a candle, Roman or otherwise, to the bombs bursting in air over the Washington Mall or the 1812 Overture booming along the banks of the Charles. You didn't get that big a bang out of Bethel, but you didn't have to fight a million people to get home. Sometimes, less was more.

Until Crandall called, Maine was where I intended to be on July 4, 1994. Crandall was Ruth's roommate from college, and every year she made her husband, Erskine, and their three children go on a family trip. To quell dissent, each family member was allowed to bring one friend. Crandall and Erskine would bring Ruth and me. These trips were usually in August and always a lot of fun. Crandall was a great planner. One year she had us hiking through the Cascades in Washington, another, floating down the Salmon River in Idaho. This year, Crandall had booked a bicycle trip through the wine country of France. But the only time everyone could make it was the second week of July.

Normally, I'd have said no. I like July in Maine. Plus, I have no desire to go anyplace where they don't speak English. I have a tin ear and have spent my whole life being frustrated by languages. Ruth, on the other hand, has a tremendous ear. She is fluent in Spanish, can read French, and understands Italian. Ruth's ear is so good, she can name almost any popular tune after hearing just three notes. I, on the other hand, can listen to a whole song and never be able to hum a bar. It was Ruth's ear that made France a possibility. We'd gone to Mexico that winter, and thanks to Ruth I had a wonderful time. With her interpreting, I could order food, ask questions, even tell jokes. Plus, this trip to France had a silver lining: that fall would mark our twenty-fifth wedding anniversary.

I not only agreed to go, I decided we'd go a week early. Ruth had toured Europe when she was in college and loved it. I'd never been to the Continent. I figured we could spend a week in Paris basking in the Enlightenment before meeting Crandall and her troops in Dijon. A week in the City of Light would be my silver wedding anniversary gift to Ruth.

●   ●   ●

On June 28, we boarded Air France Flight 23 at Washington/ Dulles and flew through the night to Paris/de Gaulle. A friend had offered us an apartment in Paris near the Gare de l'Est. Because the apartment was so near the station, our friend told us to take the train in from the airport. "It'll save you a ton of money," she said, "and the trains are fun."

We claimed our bags, caught the shuttle bus, and arrived at the airport train station at 8 A.M., right at the height of the morning rush hour. The de Gaulle station was a beehive of activity. Announcements were blaring over the loudspeaker. *"Reims, Reims, le train quarante-huit, la voie neuf." "Senlis, Senlis, le train soixante-sept, la voie douze." "Paris, Paris, le train cent soixante-deux, la voie seize. Madames, Messieurs, a voiture, s'il vous plait!"*

"What'd they say? What'd they say?" I barked at Ruth. "I heard the word *Paris*. That must be our train."

They're talking too fast," Ruth said. "I can't understand them." She looked confused. This was not good.

I grabbed a passing commuter. "Pardon, mizzure, my Madame wants to ask you a question."

"Oui?"

"¿Cual tren va a Paris, por favor?" What? Even my tin ear could tell that Ruth was not speaking French.

"Pardonnez-moi, Madame, je ne parle pas l'espagnol." The confused commuter darted off.

"Ruth, what are you doing?" I growled. "Speak French!"

"I can't. My Spanish has taken over."

"Oh, great. Here we are starting two weeks in France, and you suddenly decide you can't speak French. Ruth, what are you doing to me?" She didn't say a thing. The always talkative Ruth had gone mute.

On our first night in gay Paree, our friend Peggy took us on a walking tour of the Palais Royal, the Louvre, and the Palais de Justice. The whole Continent was locked in a massive heat wave, and the city was suffocating. We finally stopped at a sidewalk cafe in the shadow of Notre Dame. I was ready for a drink. All these college kids were sitting around with huge steins of beer. Given the heat, a big beer looked delicious. I ordered one, chugged it down, and ordered another. When the bill came, I nearly fell into the Seine. The beers were twenty dollars—apiece!

How could these college kids be drinking twenty-dollar beers? Daddy's credit card had them living in a fantasy world. It was Thursday night. I thought to myself, why am I stuck in this hot city with a bunch of spoiled kids paying twenty dollars a beer when I could be at Westways with real people sucking down a five-dollar six-pack of Sam Adams?

Three days in the City of Light was enough for me. With every air conditioner in Paris working overtime, the Enlightenment was suffering a brownout. I'd been in enough museums and seen enough paintings to last me a lifetime. I looked at Monet's *Water Lilies* and thought of Sucker Brook. Manet's *Luncheon on the Grass* reminded me of a picnic supper on the Bethel Town Common. Courbet's *Stonebreakers* were dead ringers for Rodney, Titian's *Man with a Glove* embodied the spirit of a young Reverend Jordan, and Whistler's mother could have been any one of the Stone sisters. Silver anniversary or no silver anniversary, I wished I was in Maine.

On our third night, Peggy threw us a party with a group of expatriates. Everybody was standing around sweating and talking about the weather. They all told us what fools we were to stay in Paris when we didn't have to. "Get out to the countryside," they said.

"Where?"

"Anywhere. Brittany, Normandy, Burgundy, the Loire Valley."

Since Brittany and Normandy were in the wrong direction

and we were going to Burgundy with Crandall, the general consensus was that we should tour the château country of the Loire Valley.

"How will we find places to stay?" I said.

"*Pas de probleme,*" they assured us. "There are scenic little inns all over France." Peggy pulled out a Michelin guide. "Here," she said, opening it up. "You can leave tomorrow morning, drive to Chartres, tour the cathedral, have lunch, then take a leisurely ride to the château country."

"Isn't the Loire like the Mississippi?" I said. "Doesn't it run right through the heart of France's industrial center? I don't want to be playing in Peoria." That got a laugh. Imagine anyone confusing the Loire Valley with Peoria.

"Don't worry. We'll get you off to a good start," said Peggy. She started thumbing through the guide. "Ah, here we go, Beaugency. *Parfait.* Listen to this. 'A clutch of historic towers and buildings around a fourteenth-century bridge.' And here's a little *auberge* at a reasonable price." She picked up the phone and dialed a number. There was a quick conversation in French. The only word I understood was "Morine." "*D'accord,*" Peggy said, hanging up. "Well, you're off to the château country."

I was the driver, Ruth the navigator. Leaving Paris, we had a few skirmishes finding the "bd. Pèriphèrique" and making the turnoff onto the A10 south, but the real battle came when A10 split into A10 and A11. All Frenchmen drive like they're running the Le Mans. Our little rental Renault was pushing seventy-five just trying to keep up with the normal flow of traffic. "Okay," I said to Ruth, my hands glued to the wheel, "the highway's about to divide. Which lane do we want, right or left?"

"Er, um, er." Ruth was wrestling with the Michelin map, a big, unwieldy blur of green and white crisscrossed with red and yellow lines.

"Come on, come on, let's go! Right or left?" A truck roared by the Renault on the right. I swerved left. Ruth was still fumbling with the Michelin, but I could now see a sign pointing to Chartres on the right. I tried to change lanes. A Camembert cheese truck blew its horn and drove me back. Too late; we'd missed the turn.

Ruth and I are excellent travelers when somebody else has planned the trip. We're always upbeat, never complain, and are very funny. When something goes wrong, we're the first to see the humor in it. For years, Nature Conservancy people asked us to come along on trips with major donors. They knew that Ruth and I had the ability to turn the worst debacle into the most memorable experience, and often we did.

Traveling by ourselves is different. Neither one of us likes to make a decision. Once a decision is made, we tend to second-guess each other, and when something goes wrong, we're quick to blame. This combination of crummy characteristics came to light on our ride to Beaugency. "Ruth, I give you one simple job and you screw it up." "You were driving like a maniac." "I had no choice. Did you see those trucks?" "You should have gotten off at the next exit." "Why? So you could miss another turn?" Anyone sitting in the back seat would have wondered how we'd ever made it to our silver anniversary. I was beginning to wonder myself.

As we steamed down A10, two huge cooling towers from a nuclear reactor loomed. "Look at that," I said. "A nuclear power plant. I knew the Loire River Valley was an industrial center."

"Don't worry," Ruth said. "I'm sure they'd never put a power plant next to a scenic village."

Wrong again. The power plant hovered over Beaugency like a fiery dragon. When we took a walk along the Loire, the banks of the river were riprapped and covered with dead fish, undoubtedly victims of thermal pollution. The charm of the fourteenth-century bridge was completely overshadowed by the transmission towers, and thanks to all the power lines, the village's historic towers looked more like giant clothespins. Beaugency had been hung out to dry. Next to it, Peoria didn't seem so bad.

"How could the people in this village let the government build a power plant right on top of them?" I said. "I can tell you one thing, this never would have happened in Lovell."

I was right. Back in the eighties, the Nuclear Regulatory Commission (NRC) was trying to find a place to store all the spent nuclear rods being produced by America's atomic power plants. Because western Maine is mostly granite and not prone to earthquakes, the NRC figured it could find some mountain, carve it out, and dump the rods there. Given the fact that western Maine is so sparsely populated, the NRC didn't think it would run up against much opposition. That was a mistake.

When the plan for the toxic waste dump became public, people in Lovell and the surrounding towns quickly mobilized. Physicists, other scientists, writers, artists, and just plain people joined together and formed an alliance to fight the project. This alliance was so smart, so well prepared, and so determined that Congress eventually decided America's nuclear waste would be better off buried under the desert in New Mexico. Obviously, the citizens of Beaugency lacked the fortitude of Mainers.

The next day, we started touring castles. Once I'd seen one, I'd seen them all. What really burned me was Château de Bois. It cost an arm and a leg to tour these places, and when we got inside the Château de Bois, we discovered that most of the castle was closed for renovation. Basically, all that was open was the sun-beaten courtyard and the gift shop. "Who do these frogs think they're kidding?" I said, pulling out our tickets. "I wasn't born yesterday. I'm getting our francs back."

I stormed the ticket office. The ticket man saw me coming.

He threw up a sign and slammed the window shut. *"Fermé pour le déjeuner."* I pounded on the window. A little peephole slid open. "You charge us full price when most of the castle's closed?" I said, trying to stuff the tickets through the peephole. "I want my money back."

"Nous sommes fermé pour le déjeuner. Vous pouvez revenir en deux heures." This was the same guy who was chatting Ruth up when we'd bought the tickets, asking her where she'd gotten her shoes. Now, he couldn't speak a word of English.

"Ruth, help me out here," I said.

"They're closed for lunch," she said. "You can come back in two hours."

"Two hours? I'm not hanging around this dump for two hours. Tell this crook we want our francs back, and we want them now."

Ruth turned and walked away. The scene at the airport train station had knocked the wind out of her linguistic sails. She refused to speak any French. In Ruth's defense, the French were arrogant. When we were in Mexico, everybody was encouraging and helpful when she spoke Spanish. It didn't make any difference how bad she sounded. In France, they looked down their noses at the slightest mistake. That was their loss; I didn't get to tell one joke the whole time we were in France.

"Let's get out of here," I said, throwing the tickets on the ground. "I'm sick of the Loire."

"Where do you want to go?" Ruth asked.

"We'll try one of the tributaries, the Cher or the Indre. They might be cooler," I said. "And maybe the people there will be a little nicer," I shouted, making sure the ticket guy heard me. I hoped he choked on his croissant.

We found a small but architecturally pleasing château in a little village on the Indre. It was surrounded by beautiful gardens and at one time must have been a real showplace. It had been given to some national preservation organization by the heirs of the original count. Unfortunately, the preservation organization had seen the gift of this remote château as a way to make a few extra francs and had subdivided the grounds around the château into mini-estates. So what if these new homes compromised the integrity of the château and destroyed the ambiance of the village? Let them eat cake, I can hear the preservation organization saying.

The same thing almost happened in Lovell. In the early 1900s, Robert Eastman of Chicago was president of W.F. Hall, the largest printer of catalogs in the world. Eastman's family was originally from Lovell. In 1912, Robert repurchased the family farm on the top of Eastman Hill and turned it into the Eastman Hill Stock Farm, so named because that's where he raised champion horses and cattle. The stock farm was to Robert Eastman what Westways was to William Armstrong Fairburn, a grand summer estate on which no expense was spared.

The stock farm consists of a gorgeous brick Federal-style home with an attached clapboard barn that Eastman transformed into a medieval hall. Along with the main house and barn there's a farm manager's house, a working barn, and a caretaker's cottage. All of these buildings have fabulous views and are surrounded by lush lawns, sculptured gardens, well-pruned orchards, rolling fields, and weathered fieldstone walls. This three-hundred-acre estate is the pride of all Lovell. Locals and summer folk like to drive up Eastman Hill to admire the grounds and the buildings, which are always meticulously maintained. The stock farm could hold its own with just about anything in château country, and nothing in all of France could beat its views.

In 1989, Robert Eastman's daughter died and left the stock farm, along with an $800,000 endowment, to the National Trust for Historic Preservation. The town of Lovell was delighted. Now the estate would get the national recognition it so well deserved. Professionals from the trust began flying in. Studies were done, documentations made, a preliminary report prepared. The report concluded that the Eastman Hill Stock Farm was "not of museum quality." Such being the case, the National Trust planned to place restrictions on the buildings, sell them off with a few acres, then subdivide the rest of the property into mini-estates. The proceeds would go into the National Trust's Historic Preservation Properties Fund and be used to help maintain other properties. As for the endowment, by the time the studies were done, it was half gone.

When Howard Corwin, the head of the Greater Lovell Land Trust, got wind of the plan, he went ballistic. Howard, a retired psychiatrist who volunteers the bulk of his time to the land trust, had little patience with stupidity, insincerity, and politics. At Eastman Hill, the land trust confronted all three: a plan that clearly would not protect the land, a national organization that seemed to be paying lip service to local concerns, and an endowment that appeared to have been managed in a Machiavellian manner.

Seeing Howard's rage, the town was no longer awed by the National Trust for Historic Preservation. Many of the same people who had joined forces to defeat the atomic waste dump began to use their considerable talents to rally support for the stock farm. Articles critical of the National Trust began to appear in the local and national press. Tough questions were asked regarding the studies and the report. The endowment was placed under great scrutiny.

Because of this support, the Greater Lovell Land Trust and the town were able to forge a compromise with the National Trust. The stock farm was preserved in total, and what was left of the endowment was put in a fund that would be used to benefit only the property and the town. Unlike the Frenchmen in this little village on the Indre, the people of Lovell weren't going to let one of their jewels be cut up and sold to shine somebody else's tiara. They weren't going to eat cake.

I'd had it with the Loire Valley, the château country, the heat, and the development. "We're heading to the mountains," I said.

"What mountains?" Ruth said.

"The Alps."

"Are you crazy? That's three hundred miles from here."

"Well, you wanted to see France."

We drove and we drove. Orleans and the triumph of Jeanne d'Arc, Bourges and its Cathédrale St. Étienne, Nevers and its earthenware, Charolais and its white cattle, Fuissé and its white wine. We pressed on. The rolling hills around Mâcon suggested that we were approaching the Alps. By now it was the Fourth of July and we were sweltering in our non–air-conditioned Renault. "I'm hungry," Ruth said. "Pick a place and let's stop for lunch."

I pulled into a roadside stand with some tables out front. Ruth was amazed when the proprietress, a plump and pleasant peasant, offered us twelve different varieties of homegrown snails. I would have traded all twelve snails for one red hot dog. "What is it you want?" Ruth demanded.

"I want a little house with window boxes on a crystal clear lake that looks into the mountains. That's what I want."

"That's Maine," Ruth said. "Get a grip on yourself. We're in France." In desperation, she broke her silence. In halting French, she asked the proprietress if she knew of a lake where we could go swimming.

"*Oui, Madame,*" the proprietress gushed enthusiastically. "*Il y a un grand lac seulement trente kilometres d'ici.*"

Ruth wrote down the directions. We paid our bill and headed north, away from the Alps but toward the Monts Jura, the range that forms the border between France and Switzerland. I was encouraged. We were gaining altitude and entering a deep forest. Right away, it felt cooler. "This lake looks promising," I said, "very promising."

We saw a sign: *La nage—1 km.* Ruth checked her directions. "This is it," she said proudly.

We turned the corner and were faced with a sea of cars. Beyond the parking lot were thousands of fat French in skimpy black Speedos packed around a little pond, all sweating, talking, eating, and drinking. The beach was so crowded that one person had to stand up before another could sit down. Neither Ruth nor I said a word. We'd made so many bad decisions and second-guessed each other so often that, at this point, assigning blame was a waste of time.

I gave the Renault a goose and drove blindly into the Monts Jura. Late that afternoon, we pulled into the Grand Hotel de la Poste, the only hotel still operating in Morez, the last town in France. Morez had seen better days, probably when Napoleon was emperor. It reminded me of Berlin, as in Berlin, New Hampshire: dirty, dumpy, and played out. The Grand Hotel de la Poste was no longer grand. It was old, seedy, and, as far as I could tell, empty.

I asked for the best room. The porter, dressed in a strappy T-shirt to beat the heat, showed us a suite. The threadbare carpet and torn lace curtains hinted at a more prosperous past, but the room was stuffy, the air musty. The porter threw open the big casement windows. Below, I could hear the babbling of a mountain brook. For an instant, I was transported to Maine. I was standing on the log dam at the end of Horseshoe Pond listening to the crystal clear water spill into Sucker Brook Then I looked down and saw a fetid stream rolling over a truck tire. I was back in Morez.

That evening, as we sat by ourselves in the main dining

room of the Grand Hotel de la Poste, I stared at the menu hoping to find a "Rouge Hot Dog à la Jordan." Ruth was so depressed that, once again, she'd gone mute. Not only wouldn't she speak French, she wouldn't even read it, at least not to me. I'd have to fend for myself. In desperation, I ordered the house special, tripe. Something in the far recesses of my mind told me tripe came in a casing, like a hot dog. It might even be red. What arrived was pink and rubbery, foul looking, foul smelling, and foul tasting. Worse yet, I had no one to blame but myself.

On the evening of July 4, 1994, in the twenty-fifth year of our marriage, we had reached the low point of our silver anniversary trip. I pushed away the foul-looking, foul-smelling, foul-tasting tripe, raised my glass of cheap wine, and said, "Never again will I spend another Fourth of July in any place but Maine."

ALWAYS
LEAVE THE KEYS
WITH THE CAR

Given our blunders on Baldface, I never thought I'd see Skipper Tonsmeire back in Maine, but the very next year he suggested another trip to the cabin. "I'd like Dan to see that foliage," Skipper said. Dan was one of Skipper's seven younger brothers. "And we can take that canoe ride down the Saco." We'd never gotten to go canoeing on the Saco River the previous year. The morning after our climb on Baldface, Lois had insisted that we drive her to the Portland Jetport. She'd seen enough of Maine. After meeting the real Mother Nature, Lois wanted to get back to L.A., where it was warm and safe.

"No problem," I told Skipper. "I'll pick you up at the jetport."

Skipper and Dan arrived in Portland on the first Friday of October. It was a classic fall day: sunny, warm, and windless. The leaves were at their peak. As we zipped along Route 113 through the hills of Hiram and Brownfield, Skipper and Dan marveled at the reds, oranges, and iridescent golds shimmering in the autumn light. "Look at those colors," Skipper said. "I believe those trees are 'bout the prettiest I've ever seen."

I slowed down as we passed a particularly spectacular sugar maple beside a weathered red barn. "You haven't seen anything yet," I said. "Wait 'til we get to the lake."

They were not disappointed. When we pulled up to the cabin, Kezar was a mirror reflecting a blaze of color. Skipper and Dan immediately wanted to launch the canoe. "No, not yet," I said. "You can't appreciate the lake until you've seen the view from Hilltop Farm. Plus, I want to pick up some vegetables for dinner."

Hilltop Farm worked on the honor system. Everything that had survived the first frost had been picked and piled on Hilltop Farm's front porch. While Skipper and Dan gazed into the Presidential Range, I grabbed a bag and began rummaging through the squash, onions, zucchini, and tomatoes. I was hoping to find a few ears of corn, but corn never survives the first frost. When I had what I wanted, I studied the price list tacked to the screen door, dropped a five-dollar bill into the big wicker basket, and counted out my change. "Damn, there must be forty dollars in there," Dan said, looking in the basket. "Seems like this guy's 'bout ripe to get picked himself."

"What do you think, all Yankees are crooks?" I said. "You know, people in Maine are as nice as they are in Mobile." Skipper and Dan gave me a dubious look. They obviously didn't expect to find honor in any system north of the Mason-Dixon.

When we got back to the cabin, Skipper and Dan immediately dragged the *Ruda* out from under the porch. "We can paddle up Sucker Brook," I suggested. "Who knows, we might see a moose."

It was clear that Dan and Skipper figured I was pulling their leg. They'd seen moose on the rivers out west, but Kezar Lake wasn't any wilderness. There were cabins all over the place. "Come on, boy, stop tryin' to impress us," Skipper drawled. "We've seen pretty trees, and even an honest Yankee, but we're not gonna see a moose. This lake ain't wild enough for moose."

"Well, I've never seen one," I had to admit, "but people say they're around."

At dusk, Sucker Brook was alive with wildlife moving in for the night. Flocks of ducks circled warily before setting their wings and gliding into the marsh. A great blue heron flew up the brook ahead of us, squawking a warning that we were coming. A little mink apparently didn't hear the heron. It dove out of sight when we surprised it as we paddled around a bend. A muskrat lugging a big branch back to its den wasn't so cautious. It kept swimming right by the canoe, too busy to be bothered by the likes of us. Nature was putting on a great show, except the star was missing. We saw no moose.

By the time we got back to the dock, the sun had set behind our old nemeses, the Baldfaces, and the bright oranges, reds, and golds covering the mountains were melding to a hazy purple. In the twilight, the first stars were beginning to twinkle. It was going to be a beautiful night. We'd gotten three juicy New York strips at the Center Lovell Store and were going to cook them outside over a campfire. "I'll start the fire while you cut up those vegetables," Skipper said to Dan and me.

"Okay," I said, "but first I'm putting on something warm."

As the perfect host, I'd taken the Tonsmeire boys to L.L. Bean's. They'd bought some Gore-Tex/Thinsulate Wintersport gloves, and I'd found a deal on a Polartec fleece pullover. With the sun down, it was getting cold, so I pulled on the Polartec. I'd learned my lesson on Baldface. You can't trust fall weather in Maine, and I wasn't going to get caught cold again.

A heavy mist hung over the lake the next morning. When I sat up in my bunk and looked out the window, I could hardly see the water. The Tonsmeire boys were lying out on the porch in their sleeping bags. Unlike me, the Tonsmeires liked to rough it. I climbed out of my soft bunk, took a nice hot shower, stoked up the fire, poured myself a cup of coffee, put on the Polartec, and went out to join them. I had just sat down when we heard heavy breathing coming from the lake.

"What's that?" Dan said.

"I don't know," I said. I'd never heard anything like it.

There was sloshing and splashing. Something was coming across the lake right towards us, and it sounded big. We jumped up as two moose, a bull and a cow, clambered out of the water and strode past the porch. They weren't more than fifteen yards away. "Wail, I'll be damned," Skipper said, "the boy went out and rented us some moose."

Watching the sun burn the mist off the lake reminded me of a Polaroid developing. First came the opposite shore, then the hills, then the mountains. By 10 A.M., we had the whole picture, another perfect fall day. "'Bout time for a swim," Skipper said.

This time, I didn't hesitate. I never thought I'd have a swim as good as the one we'd had the year before, but this was just as good, if not better. We swam and swam. I couldn't get enough of the mountains, the colors, the water. Then, when I was sure that things couldn't get any better, a group of eight loons paddled over and began diving for fish all around us. "I don't believe I've ever seen anything like that before," Dan said.

"Skipper, what do you think?" I kidded. "Those moose must have stirred up some fish for the loons."

After a delicious lunch at the Wicked Good, the local one-stop, we headed down Route 5 to Fryeburg. We were going to spend the afternoon canoeing the Saco, and then I planned to give the Tonsmeire boys another treat. I was going to introduce them to Clyde Darling, Fryeburg's most famous fishmonger. For the last twenty-five years, Clyde had been selling lobsters from his camper at the junction of Routes 5 and 113, opposite the monument to John Stevens. I knew that the Tonsmeires would enjoy meeting this local landmark, and Dan's first trip to Maine wouldn't be complete without cracking into a lobster.

As the Saco River leaves the valley, it bends around Fryeburg and sets its course to the sea. This twenty-mile scenic and sandy loop around Fryeburg is the most popular stretch of river in New England. For most of the summer, it's a zoo. During July and August, more than 150,000 canoers paddle the loop. Canoes are stacked up like bumper cars, many of them loaded with beer and blaring rock music. The Saco in summer is Maine's answer to the Jersey Shore. I'd never take serious outdoorsmen like the Tonsmeires on it then, but in October I figured we'd have the river pretty much to ourselves.

Since we were only going for the afternoon, I decided we'd do just the second half of the loop. We'd put in at the Canal Bridge on Route 5 and take out at the public landing on Lovewell Pond. I'd leave the car at the Canal Bridge and bum a ride back to get it after we'd taken out. As we unloaded the *Ruda* at the Canal Bridge parking lot and got ready to leave, Skipper took the keys to the rental car and tucked them under the left front tire.

"I think we'd better take the keys with us," I said. "I don't trust some of the people who use this lot."

"Y'all sure?" Skipper said. "Down south, we always leave the keys with the car."

"I'm sure you do," I said, zipping the keys into my pack. "But not everyone on the Saco recognizes the honor system."

The first seven miles on the Saco were as nice as any I'd ever spent on a river. The sun was high and hot. It was so warm that we took our shirts off. When Skipper spied a rope hanging from an old pine leaning over the river, he guided the canoe into shore. "Let's give that swing a try," he said.

Skipper and Dan looked like Flying Wallendas as they swung out to the very end of the rope, let go, did a flip, and dove into the Saco. "Git that rope, boy," Skipper said to me. "This is your river."

I struggled up the trunk of the old pine tree, grabbed the rope, and pushed off. *Flump.* I dropped straight into the water. When I came up, Dan said, "Ya gotta hang on. Come on, give it another try."

"No thanks," I said, climbing back into the *Ruda.* I knew I wasn't strong enough to swing with the Tonsmeires.

When we rounded the next bend, we surprised a young couple necking on the bank. Unlike the little mink at Sucker Brook, they couldn't dive under the water, even though I'm sure that's what they wanted to do. Instead, they gave us a sheepish wave. We nodded politely and paddled on. Once we were out of earshot, I said, "Seeing those kids reminds me of my first kiss. It happened right here on the Saco. I'll show you the spot when we pass it."

"Who was she?" Skipper asked.

"A girl on Lovewell Pond. Her parents had a place right near where we're going to take out."

"How old were ya?" Dan said.

"Fifteen," I said. "We were staying at Jordan's Camps. The other kids had gone off to climb Pleasant Mountain. I had an ear infection so I couldn't go with them. I was sitting on the beach looking for them to shine a mirror from the top of the moun-tain—that's what we used to do, shine a mirror back to camp once we got to the top—when this girl pulls up. Brenda was her name. She was a friend of the Jordan girls. It was their dad who owned the camps. All the guys at Jordan's liked Brenda. She had a speedboat and wore a little bikini."

"Sounds like a good girl," Skipper said.

"No question you would've liked her," I said. "Anyway, since none of the other kids were around, she asked me if I wanted to go for a ride. I said, sure, why not, and off we went down the lake. When we came to the outlet, she asked me if I wanted to go down to the Saco. Brenda was a year or so older than I was, and a lot more experienced, so I was getting a little nervous, but I figured, why not? This could be the chance of a lifetime.

"It was real hot, and when we got to the river Brenda pulled the boat up on a sandbank; she wanted to go for a swim. I told her I couldn't swim because of my ear, so she suggested we sit in the sand with our feet in the water. The next thing I know, she's got her tongue about halfway down my throat and I'm really liking it. Then I hear all this hooting and hollering. I look up and there's a whole line of Boy Scouts going by. It's some troop on a canoe trip. We were like that couple back there, only the Boy Scouts gave us all kinds of crap. There was nothing I could do but sit there and take it. It was really embarrassing."

"What did Brenda do?" Dan said.

"Now, Brenda, she was smart. She took a towel and put it over her head. She was laughing the whole time. If I hadn't known better, I'd have sworn she planned it."

"You're lucky to have ended up with Ruth," Skipper said.

"You're not the first to have made that observation."

"And I won't be the last."

About three o'clock, we came to Walker's Bridge, the point where the Saco crosses under Route 302. I was surprised to see a long line of cars backed up across the bridge. Then I remembered: this was the last day of the Fryeburg Fair, "Maine's Blue Ribbon Classic." The fair must have been experiencing a record crowd, and for us that presented a problem.

"Pull in here," I said to Skipper and Dan. "With all that traffic heading to the fair, we're going to have trouble getting back to the car. Why don't you let me out here. That way, I can bum back to the car and meet you at the Lovewell landing."

"How do we get to the pond?" Skipper said.

"Just follow the river for another five miles or so. The outlet from Lovewell comes in on the right. There'll be a sign tacked to a tree pointing towards the pond, but don't miss it. The next takeout is Brownfield, and that's another four miles. You wouldn't make it until after dark."

"See ya at Lovewell," Skipper said, pushing off.

I watched them round the bend past the bridge, then scrambled up the bank to the road. The traffic was barely moving. I stuck out my thumb, but all I got were strange looks. Then it occurred to me that I'd forgotten my shirt. Here I was, standing by the side of the road in Maine in October dressed in a bathing suit. No wonder I was getting all these strange looks.

I started jogging towards Fryeburg. Jogging wasn't a bad idea. It legitimized my dress and I was chugging along faster than the traffic. By the time I reached the convenience store at Jockey Cap, on the outskirts of Fryeburg, I'd run more than two miles, so I decided to treat myself to a beer.

I walked into the store, grabbed a frosty Moosehead from the cooler, and went up to the counter, but when I reached into my pocket, there was nothing but some sand from the Saco. "Oh, no," I said to the clerk. "I forgot my wallet." Then it dawned on me. I'd forgotten my pack. "Dammit!" I bellowed. "I don't have the keys to the car."

I had to find the Tonsmeires, which meant I had to get to the public landing on Lovewell. That was another six miles, way too far for me to jog. I'd have to bum a ride. I sprinted down the road that runs behind Fryeburg Academy. It connected Route 302 to 113, the main route to Portland and the road to the landing on Lovewell. There was a football game going on at the academy. I could see the fans standing around the field in their sweaters and coats. Suddenly I felt cold. Clouds were rolling in over the Presidential Range, and the temperature was dropping like a rock. I began to shiver. The real Mother Nature was up to her old tricks. Like a lot of women, she seemed to enjoy following Skipper around.

When I got to Route 113, it began to drizzle. I stuck out my thumb and prayed somebody would stop. Nobody did. Who in Maine was going to pick up some nut in a bathing suit standing by the side of the road, in the rain, in October? Cars actually sped up as they passed me. I looked down 113 to John Stevens' monument. Through the drizzle, I could see that Clyde Darling's camper was gone. Clyde had a well-publicized penchant for the ponies, so he must have packed up early and headed for the races at the fair. There would be no lobsters tonight, but lobsters were the least of my worries. Unless I could find a ride, the Tonsmeires would be waiting wet and hungry at the landing at Lovewell Pond.

I started walking along 113. At the first house, a guy was pulling out of the driveway in his pickup. A big black Lab sat in the cab next to him. "Excuse me," I said, "but could you give me a lift to the town landing on Lovewell?"

The Lab growled, but the guy was a bit kinder. "Ayuh. S'pose you could get in the back."

It was raining harder. Water spattered off the roof of the cab onto my blue body. I thought of my nice warm Polartec sitting back at the cabin. Was I ever going to learn? The guy let me out by the road that led down to the landing. The Lab was still growling. I thanked the guy and started staggering down the road. My whole body had gone numb. I prayed that the Tonsmeires would be sitting under the *Ruda* waiting for me. They weren't. I stumbled out onto the rocks and surveyed the pond. It looked cold, deserted, and dark. Now what? No keys, no car, no money, no clothes, no canoe, and no Tonsmeires. They must have missed the turn and gone on to Brownfield.

I plopped down under a tree. There was nothing I could do.

I didn't know where to go, and even if I did, how would I get there? It was raining even harder. The nearest public phone was in Fryeburg, five miles away. Even then, who would I call? How had this day turned so bad? By now, we should have been sitting in my warm, cozy cabin beside a roaring fire, dipping big chunks of Clyde Darling's lobster into a dish of melted butter. If only I'd listened to Skipper and left the keys with the car.

I was jolted out of my misery by the sound of a canoe coming into the landing. I jumped up. "Skipper! Dan! Where the hell have you been?"

"Eatin' lobster," Skipper said.

"What?"

"People up here sure are nice," Dan said.

"What people?"

"The ones that took us in," Skipper said. "We was sittin' here in the rain, waitin' on you, when these people come by and invited us to their camp. They'd just bought a bunch of lobsters from some guy down in Fryeburg. Got 'em just before he closed."

"Boy, they sure were good," Dan added. "But what really topped it off was that blueberry pie and ice cream."

Right then, a pickup pulled into the landing. An elderly couple got out. "Hey, Skipper, Dan. Is that your friend?"

"That's him," Skipper said.

"Well, throw the canoe in the truck and we'll drive you back to your car. Say," the guy said, looking at me, "you ought to put on a coat and some long pants. You're not in Alabama, you know."

That night, as I picked through what was left of the vegetables, Skipper and Dan were lying in front of the fire rehashing the day. "Y'all sure did show us a good time," Dan said.

"My pleasure," I said, chucking a burned zucchini into the fire.

"Too bad you missed that lobster and blueberry pie," Skipper said. "But like I told ya, down south we always leave the keys with the car."

RIGHT IN THE
HEART OF MAINE

Social Security is a wonderful thing. If you can reach sixty-five with some savings, no debt, and modest needs, Social Security goes a long way towards providing financial freedom. Dad stopped worrying about money once he started receiving Social Security. It was as if he'd been running a financial marathon all his adult life and finally crossed the finish line. Social Security, along with some very sound investments, turned the rest of Dad's life into one long, enjoyable victory lap.

Social Security had a similar effect on Rodney, only money wasn't his major worry. For Rodney, it was time. Given his wide range of interests, Rodney's days were too short. Once he started receiving his monthly check from Uncle Sam, his days suddenly got longer. Instead of working, Rodney would be sailing, fishing, traveling, or spending a whole week at the Fryeburg Fair. It wasn't that he was retired, but thanks to Social Security, work was no longer a priority.

For that reason, I wasn't surprised when Rodney called one

Tuesday morning and asked if I wanted to go canoeing. I was hoping he was calling to tell me that he'd finally finished a corner cupboard he'd been promising Ruth for the past five years, but no such luck. It was too nice a day for Rodney to be thinking about corner cupboards. "I'll get out the eighteen-footer," he said. "Be nice on the Androscoggin. Ayuh." The eighteen-footer was a big Old Town canoe that Rodney had picked up on a deal somewhere. The field behind Rodney's house was cluttered with toys he'd picked up on deals. The problem was, until Social Security, he'd never had enough time to use his toys.

"Sounds great," I said. "I'll see you in an hour."

"Was that Rodney?" Ruth asked hopefully.

"Yeah, we're going canoeing on the Androscoggin. Want to come?"

"No," she said, looking forlornly at the cardboard boxes still piled in the corner. "I've got things to do around here." Thanks to Social Security, it would be some time before Ruth saw her corner cupboard, and she knew it.

We were going to put in just below the Union Water Power dam in Shelburne, New Hampshire. Carol had driven us up to Shelburne and would pick us up fifteen miles downstream in West Bethel. We parked just below the dam and got out. I looked over the Androscoggin, taking its measure. There wasn't much to it. A trickle of water was coming over the dam, and the pool below was as calm as a millpond. The mighty Androscoggin was low and slow, more like a southern stream than a New England river. I wondered if there was enough water for us to make it.

"Ayuh, we'll have to do some paddlin' today," Rodney said, snatching the bright yellow eighteen-foot canoe off the top of the pickup and flipping it to the ground. Rodney might have been a senior citizen, but he was as strong as a bull moose. "Okay," he said, surveying the bank, "we'll walk 'er down that path over there and put 'er in just beyond the rocks."

I grabbed the bow and gave it a tug. The canoe barely budged. The old Old Town was made of canvas and wood and felt like it weighed a ton. Union Water hadn't provided a public landing as part of its Shelburne dam, and the informal path to the river was steep and rocky. As we started down, I began slipping and sliding on the loose gravel and losing my grip. I winced each time I heard the bottom of the Old Town scrape the rocks. I didn't want Rodney to think I couldn't hold up my end, especially after he'd just flipped the whole canoe off the truck by himself.

When we reached the river, it was obvious that the best way to launch was for me to wade the bow out into the river. "Hang on, Rod," I said, carefully setting the bow down on the shore. "Let me take my shoes off. They're brand new and I don't want to get them wet."

On our way north for the summer, Ruth and I had stopped at the Dexter outlet in Windham and I'd bought myself a new pair of boat shoes, Navigators, "made with extra cushioning in case you ever run aground." Ruth had given me a new pair of white woolen socks to go with them. I loved my new Navigators with the white woolen socks. They made me feel like I was back in the fifties, a kid again at Jordan's Camps. I'd been wearing the shoes and socks every day.

I kicked off the Navigators, stuffed a white wool sock in each one, and carefully placed them in the canoe. "There, that'll keep them dry." With my shoes and socks safely stowed, I guided the bright yellow bow of the Old Town into the dull tannic waters of the Androscoggin.

Despite the fact that the Androscoggin had been tamed by Union Water, I realized right away that it was still a powerful river. We'd hardly said good-bye to Carol when we were zipping through our first riffle. I hadn't been in a canoe since I'd floated the Saco with the Tonsmeires. When a half-submerged limb suddenly came rushing towards us, I froze. I didn't know what to do.

"Rod, look out!" I finally yelled. Too late. The bow rode up over the limb, the canoe tilted sharply to the left. I started to fall out.

"Lean right," Rodney said, but I was too far gone. Out I went. My bare feet went down expecting to feel a soft, sandy bottom like the Saco's, but the Androscoggin's bed was covered with hard, slippery rocks. I couldn't find a footing. When I tried to stand up, the current that had appeared so slow back at the dam kept knocking me down. In desperation, I reached back for the canoe. It had taken on a lot of water, but somehow Rodney had managed to keep it upright. Not anymore. When I grabbed the gunwale, over it went. Now Rodney and I were both in the Androscoggin.

"Grab the cooler," Rodney shouted. He wasn't about to lose his lunch. I put my feet down and luckily found a rock I could stand on. I turned to see how Rodney was doing. He was up to his waist in water, but he had the canoe by the stern and was trying to work it over to the bank. The Old Town was almost submerged, and the cooler, my paddle, and my shoes were floating lazily above it. For a moment they hung there. Then the current grabbed them and they started floating towards me.

I snagged the cooler with one hand and my paddle with the other, but the Navigators, with my white wool socks stuffed in each one, went floating by. Damn. I was so mad I hardly felt the stones bruising my feet as I stumbled ashore. I flopped on the bank and watched in frustration as my shoes and socks went bobbing down the river. I wasn't worthy of them. I was no navigator.

"Help me turn this canoe over," Rodney said. "We'll get the water out, then check the cooler."

Empty, the Old Town had felt like it weighed a ton. Full, it did weigh a ton. I don't know how Rodney ever got it to shore. With a mighty heave, we flipped it over, and when it was empty,

Rod checked the cooler. "Top stayed tight," he said, happy to have saved his lunch. "With any luck, we might even find ya shoes. Those socks were keeping 'em up."

"Ha," I grumped. "With my luck, we'll only find one."

And that's exactly what happened. When we came to the end of the riffle, there was one shoe with one sock floating slowly down the Androscoggin.

"The other musta hit a branch and got sucked under," Rodney said.

"I knew it," I growled, scooping up the one Navigator. "And I just bought them at Dexter's. Now I'm out fifty bucks."

"Those shoes went for a hundred?" Rodney said.

"No, forty-nine ninety-five. They were on sale."

"The way I see it, ya're only out twenty-five."

"How do you figure that?"

"Well, ya only lost one shoe, and Dexter's a good company. Located in Dexter, right in the haht of Maine. Ayuh, seems like to me they'd sell ya one shoe."

Poor Rod. Good thing he's on Social Security; he must be losing it. One shoe, ha. Didn't he realize that in this day and age nobody was going to sell you just one shoe. I felt like throwing the Navigator and the one sock we'd rescued back in the river, but that would be littering. Instead, I started paddling. We had a long way to go, and I was sick of the Androscoggin.

The next day, I was sitting on the porch looking at my lone Navigator when I said out loud, "What the heck, it won't hurt to give it a try." I got up and went to the phone.

"What won't hurt?" Ruth asked.

"I'm going to see if Dexter will sell me one shoe," I said, dialing the number. "Rodney said that they're a good company, right in the heart of Maine."

Ruth gave me a skeptical look. "Ha," she huffed. "Nobody's going to sell you one shoe." So much for Rodney.

The phone rang. I asked for customer relations. "Hi, this is Kathy," a perky voice said. "How may I help ya?"

"Kathy," I said, "I have a problem." I proceeded to pour out my story. I told Kathy how I'd just bought my new Navigators at the Dexter outlet in Windham, and how I'd gone canoeing with Rodney and lost one shoe in the Androscoggin, and how Rodney had told me that Dexter was a good company, located right in the heart of Maine, and how he was sure they'd replace the shoe.

"Gee, I'm sorry," Kathy said, "but we can't replace one shoe. All our shoes are made in pairs."

"It doesn't have to be perfect," I said. "I'd be happy with a second."

"Oh, we don't keep mismades," Kathy said emphatically.

"My wife told me I was wasting my time," I said, "but thanks anyway."

I was about to hang up when Kathy said, "You just bought 'em, huh?"

"Yeah, over in Windham. Forty-nine ninety-five, on sale."

"Could ya hang on for a minute?" she asked.

"Sure," I said, wondering why.

In less than a minute, Kathy was back. "Mr. Morine," she said, "here's what we're going to do. If you'll just send me ya name and address along with the size and model number of the shoe ya lost, we'll send ya another pair for half price."

I was surprised. "Kathy, you don't have to do that," I said. "I don't deserve a new pair at half price. It's not Dexter's fault that I was stupid enough to flip over in the Androscoggin. It's not your problem. I was just hoping you might have an odd shoe."

"Sure it's our problem," Kathy said in her wonderfully perky voice. "You're a customer, and we want all our customers to feel good about their shoes. If we can't replace it, the least we can do is sell ya another pair at half price."

It'll be a few years before Social Security helps me keep my head above water, but in the meantime, I don't have to worry about my feet. Dexter's got them covered. Rodney was right. It's a good company, right in the heart of Maine.

MOOSE MAINEA

On our way from Virginia to Lovell, Ruth always insists on stopping in New Jersey to see her family. They live just outside New York City, off Exit 156 on the Garden State Parkway. We were visiting Ruth's sister Helen on our way north in '99 when I noticed my nephew Matthew, age nine, and my niece Helen Amanda, age seven, sitting in the den watching former mayor Ed Koch presiding over *The People's Court.* "It's a beautiful day," I said to Helen. "Why are those kids watching TV? They should be outside playing. Is that how they're going to spend their whole summer, glued to the boob tube?"

"They're just bored," Helen said. "We were going to the Shore to see my mother, but the traffic's bad and there's a red tide. I'll take them down tomorrow."

"The heck with that," I said. "Matthew, Helen Amanda, turn off that TV, pack your bags, and get in the car. You're going to Maine." I'd rescued Ruth from the Jersey Shore. Maybe I could do the same for the next generation.

There was some initial grumbling about missing the Fourth of July fireworks at the Jersey Shore, but Matthew and Helen Amanda had never been to Maine, and as we crawled over the George Washington Bridge, they seemed mildly enthusiastic about this unexpected adventure. When we sped across the state line into Fryeburg seven hours later, they were positively excited. They thought they'd come to the end of the earth. These two little Garden Staters had been weaned on parkways clogged with traffic and bordered by wall-to-wall developments. They couldn't believe the open roads lined with stately pines, but what really caught their eye was the big sign at the state line that read, "Welcome to Maine. Watch Out for Moose. 187 Accidents So Far This Year."

"Uncle Dave, are we going to see a moose?" asked Helen Amanda, sounding incredulous but hopeful.

"Could be," I said. "Maine's got plenty of them."

When we reached the cabin, a worried look came over their faces. "Where's the TV?" Matthew asked.

"TV?" I barked. "We're in Maine. There's no TV in Maine. We come up here to see Mother Nature, not TV."

The next day, their first in Maine, I planned to show them why Ruth and I loved the Pine Tree State. After a big breakfast of pancakes topped with real Maine maple syrup, we took them back to Horseshoe Pond. We showed them the cardinal flowers at the Sucker Brook Preserve and brought them by to meet the de La Chapelles. Matthew and Helen Amanda didn't believe that anybody could live without electricity until Pat gave them some blueberry muffins she'd cooked in Rodney's fieldstone fireplace. They were even more amazed when Dick let them paddle around the pond in a kayak he'd built. They'd never been on their own in a boat before, let alone a handmade kayak.

Back at the cabin, we had a delicious lunch of red hot dogs, then spent the afternoon on the beach soaking up the warm summer sun and swimming in the crystal clear waters of Kezar. "No red tide here," I told them.

As the sun began to set, Ruth and I put Matthew and Helen Amanda in the *Ruda* and paddled down to the marsh at the end of the lake. Before long we'd seen a loon with a chick on its back, a great blue heron, a muskrat, a pair of geese followed by a string of goslings, flocks of ducks, swarms of swallows, and a ton of turtles. When a mink swam by with her three kits, I said to the kids, "See what I mean? There's no need for TV when Mother Nature can provide a show like this."

"Yeah," Matthew said, "but when are we going to see a moose?"

After supper, we toasted marshmallows over an open fire and watched a purple haze settle over the White Mountains. When it was totally dark, I said, "Come on, we've got a surprise for you." Ruth and I walked Matthew and Helen Amanda up to the meadow at the end of the road. "There, what do you think of that?" I said, pointing to the sky.

They couldn't believe their eyes. They'd never seen so many stars. The sky was twinkling more brightly than the boardwalk at Atlantic City. "There's the Milky Way," Ruth said, pointing to the grand strand sparkling overhead. "See the Big Dipper?" I asked, pointing to the western horizon. At that moment, a meteor streaked across the sky.

"Oh, look, a shooting star," Ruth said. "Quick, make a wish. That's good luck."

"We wish we'd see a moose," Matthew and Helen Amanda chorused.

That did it. I knew that if I was going to convert these little Jerseyites into Mainers, I was going to have to find them a moose. First thing the next morning, I called Rodney. If anybody could find a moose, it was Rodney. "Ayuh," Rodney said after I'd explained the situation. "Get 'em up here 'bout five this afternoon. We'll take 'em on a moose run."

When we arrived, Rodney and Carol were cleaning out Rodney's latest toy, a big white motor home. The motor home definitely had some miles on it, but it was new to Rodney. "When did you get this thing?" I asked.

"When I turned sixty-five," Rodney said. "Figure if I'm gonna be retired, I gotta look retired."

Ruth and I introduced Matthew and Helen Amanda to Rodney and Carol, and we all piled into the RV. "You kids get up in the bunk 'bove Rodney," Carol said. "That top window's a good place for seein' moose."

Matthew and Helen Amanda scrambled into the bunk. "Mrs. Jordan, do you see many moose?" Matthew asked.

"Eighteen the other night," Carol said. "That's our record."

"At night?"

"That's when ya see 'em best, after dark when they come out to feed," Rodney said. "Catch 'em in the headlights along the side of the road. People say they like the salt."

Rodney started up the RV, and we headed for Rumford. He wanted to show the kids the Mead Paper plant, which Rodney proudly declared was "the largest paper mill under one roof in the world." The kids were not impressed. Coming from New Jersey, they'd seen plenty of big factories. What they wanted to see was a moose, but Rodney was in no hurry. It wasn't until after we had a delicious dinner at Dick's Pizza in Mexico that Rodney turned the RV onto Route 17 north.

It was a beautiful, clear evening, and Route 17 has to be one of the most scenic and unspoiled roads in Maine. The RV huffed and puffed as we followed the Swift River up through the mountains toward the Rangeleys. The kids were lying on the bunk above Rodney, their faces pressed against the window, expecting to see a moose at every turn. They were just starting to get discouraged when Rodney slowed down. "There's one," he said casually.

"Where? Where?" the kids shrieked.

"Just ahead," Rodney said, pulling in behind a couple of cars and a big green and white van parked by the edge of the road. "In the water."

About a dozen people were gathered next to a small pond dotted with lily pads. They were talking in hushed tones, taking pictures and jockeying for a better view. In the water, about twenty yards out, the huge head of a cow moose kept bobbing up and down as she fed on the bottom. Matthew and Helen Amanda jumped down from the bunk, flew out the door, and joined the group. "Be careful," Ruth yelled, but before we could stop him, Matthew was down on the shore, snapping pictures with an Instamatic Ruth had bought him.

The cow slowly munched her way across the pond, climbed out on the far side, shook herself off, and wandered into the woods. We got back into the RV and pulled onto Route 17 right behind the green and white van. "That's the Bethel Express ahead of us," Carol said. "Fella from Bethel's runnin' tours. Guarantees you'll see a moose or ya money back."

"Is he doing all right?" Ruth asked.

"'Bout full every night. He's doin' so well, there's talk of startin' another one. Moose're becomin' a big business in Bethel."

"I guess we'll be stuck with them the whole way," I grumbled. I wanted to give the kids a wilderness experience, and watching moose with a dozen other people wasn't very wild.

"They don't see 'em all," Rodney said.

As if to prove his point, we pulled over onto the gravel shoulder while the Bethel Express kept going. About fifty yards below us in a little glade well hidden from the road was a big bull feeding on some grass. "Look at those antlers!" Matthew exclaimed, grabbing his Instamatic. "Mr. Jordan, can I get out and take a picture?"

"Best to watch him from here," Rodney said. "A cow in the water's one thing, but a bull in the open, no tellin' what he might do."

There was no argument. The bull was easily the size of a draft horse, and its antlers spanned six feet. He looked like Mother Nature's version of a front-end loader, and Matthew didn't want to be the load.

By the time the bull finally sauntered off, the sun was setting and I was ready to go home. The kids had seen a bull and a cow. What more could they want?

The Bethel Express passed us coming back down 17, but much to my surprise, and Matthew and Helen Amanda's delight, Rodney kept the RV rolling north. On we went, up 17 past Byron, past the Appalachian Trail crossing, around Mooselookmeguntic—or, as Rodney told the kids, "Moose look, my gun tic"—down along Rangeley Lake to Oquossoc, onto Route 16, then up around Cupsuptic Lake, all the time seeing more and more moose. It was almost dark when we passed a sign that read, "Canada, 30 miles." This was some moose run.

At ten, we were outside Upton, going south on Route 26, when Rodney spied a bull in a bog by the side of the road. That tied the Jordans' record of eighteen moose in one night "How did you know it was there, Mr. Jordan?" Matthew asked.

"Seen 'im before. We come up this way a couple of times a week. There's lots of moose between here and Newry. Just watch for skid marks on the road. That's the easiest way to find 'em."

We were cruising along a dark and lonely stretch of 26 when the RV slowed to a crawl. "There's a mother and a calf just ahead on the left," Rodney said, angling the vehicle so the high beams were on them. We'd put the windows down and were watching when suddenly the cow lifted her huge head and perked her ears. In the blackness we could see four headlights coming our way. At first I thought it was two cars, then I heard the roar. It was four motorcycles, and they were coming fast.

The cow pranced across the road and went into the woods about twenty yards ahead of us. The calf started to follow her, then stopped in the middle of the road. I was sure we were about to see a bad accident, but Rodney began blinking his lights. There was a loud rumble as the cycles downshifted. The calf, fearing the cycles, began running towards us. We could hear its hooves clicking on the pavement as its gangly legs brought it closer and closer. I thought the calf was going to run right into the front of the RV, but at the very last moment it veered off into the woods. If I had stuck my hand out the window, I could have touched its flank.

"Wow, that was close!" Matthew exclaimed. Nobody disagreed. By blinking his lights, Rodney had saved the calf and the bikers.

We had covered 150 miles, and I was sure that Matthew and Helen Amanda would fall asleep on the ride back from Rodney's. Instead, they recounted every sighting, all twenty-one of them. It was after midnight when Ruth and I tucked them into their sleeping bags. "Well, what do you think of Maine now?" I asked.

"Maine's my favorite place in the world!" Helen Amanda proclaimed.

"Yeah, Maine's great!" Matthew agreed. "But, Uncle Dave, tomorrow do you think we can see a bear?"

GOING DEEP WITH "VIAGRA"

Whack! Another mosquito bit the dust. Things hadn't been going too well for me. My book, the one I was sure was going to be
a best-seller, had come out in April. *Whop!* By July, I'd expected
to be dining with agents, evaluating new proposals, maybe even
working on the screenplay. Instead—*thwack!*—I was sitting on
the porch of our cabin on Kezar killing mosquitoes, waiting for
the calls I now knew were never going to come. *Whap!*

"It's Thursday night," Ruth said. "Why don't you go up to
Westways and play some softball? That always picks you up."

Ruth was right. I hadn't been to Thursday night softball in a
couple of years. Maybe it would give me a lift. I packed my
cooler, grabbed my glove, and headed for the Upper Bay. As I
wound my way down the one-car lane that leads into Westways,
my spirits began to rise. When the woods opened up to reveal
William Armstrong Fairburn's precious little diamond, I felt
even better. To hell with books. It was time to play ball.

I was relieved to see so many old faces. Eddie Nista, Tom McLaughlin, Paul Armington, Angelo Campo, Mark Tripp, Steven Bennett, John Bliss, and Hopie were in the field warming up. Now in their forties, they'd lost a step or two, but I knew there were still a few great plays left in those aging bodies.

Two new faces surprised me. They belonged to women. There had always been a few women at Thursday night softball, but they were spectators seated safely on the other side of the fence. These two were on the field playing catch. I wondered whether they were just fooling around or expecting to play. Despite all of its democratic qualities, I'd never thought of Thursday night softball as part of the women's movement.

I stowed my cooler under the bench and sat down next to Angelo Campo. Angelo had lost some serious weight and had let his hair grow long. Instead of looking like a short, stocky Castro, he now favored Fabio.

"Hey, Angelo, how you doing?" I said.

"Giving it one more try, huh?" he asked.

"Yeah, I thought I'd play a few innings, but who are those girls?"

"One's Mindy; the other's Lori, Steven Bennett's wife. They've been coming every week."

"Well, at least I won't be the last pick," I said.

"Don't bet on it," Angelo said. "They're pretty good. Lori played on the all-state team in New Hampshire."

I was still studying the new faces when Tom McLaughlin came in from the field. He'd broken a sweat and was ready for a beer.

"Hey, Tom, how you doing?" I said. "Is that Ryan I see out there?" Ryan was Tom's sixteen-year-old son.

"Yeah, he's a regular now," Tom said. "Makes me feel old, but he hasn't hit one into the court yet." Like catching a bass at Jordan's, hitting one into the tennis court was the mark of manhood at Westways.

A couple of young bucks had moved aside and chosen up the teams. Now they began walking down the bench designating "ins" and "outs." "Dave, you're out," Richie said. "Why don't you take the shortfield."

Shortfield? I'd always played catcher, but Richie was a real competitor, one of the few who took Thursday night softball seriously. Richie liked to win, and while catcher batted second, shortfielder batted last. It was obvious where I stood in Richie's picks, but I didn't mind. Not catching would save my knees, and playing the shortfield might give me a chance to throw somebody out at the plate. I proved that in the first inning. A chorus of "helluva peg," "ayuh," and "not bahd for an ol' guy" echoed across the diamond when I nearly nailed Tim Chandler, a young buck with blazing speed, tagging up from third on a short fly to left.

Unfortunately, there were no choruses for my hitting. I batted after Ryan McLaughlin, who was playing right. Ryan had belted doubles in the second and fourth innings, and each time I'd left him stranded. In the second, I'd lofted a soft, lazy fly to Mindy in center, and in the fourth, Lori had robbed me. The old Ball Buster had blasted a sizzler down the first-base line, but Lori was on it like a cat. It was easy to see why she was all-state. If Lori had been playing first for the Red Sox in '86, they never would have lost the Series. Both Lori and Mindy were beautiful athletes.

On his third trip to the plate, Ryan knew better than to count on me. He smacked a high fly to left. At first I thought it was going to be caught, but the ball kept carrying. I couldn't believe it when it cleared the fence and plopped into the court. Now I really felt old. Ryan hadn't even been around when I started playing at Westways, and here he was, breaking into his first home-run trot.

I trudged over to the bat box and pulled out the Ball Buster. It had gone ashen, with crow's feet on the handle and deep wrinkles along the grain. Still, I never considered using anything else. I didn't like the ping of a metal bat. When I hit a ball, I wanted to hear the crack of a real bat like the Ball Buster.

As I was taking a few practice swings, John Bliss sidled up to me. "Hey, Dave, try this," he whispered conspiratorially. John was offering me a sleek, new, black metal bat. "We call it 'Viagra.' All the old guys are usin' it. It helps ya go deep."

Come to think of it, all the old guys *were* still giving the ball a good ride. Angelo's new Fabio physique had circled the bases twice, and Paul Armington, Mark Tripp, and Tom McLaughlin had each launched one into the court. Tom's had been a grand slam. Maybe it was time for me to reconsider my loyalty to wood.

I grabbed the bat and read the label. Viagra was a thirty-four-inch Redline model by Easton with a "Graphite Reinforced Sc500™ Alloy Shell with a Total Preen Finish." Printed on the twelve-inch "Power Contoured Barrel" was the motto "Push the Limit." I hefted Viagra in one hand, the Ball Buster in the other. "Boy, it's light," I said. "It feels terrific."

"For three hundred bucks, it oughtta," John Bliss said.

Ryan was strutting back to the bench sporting a smile that stretched from ear to ear. That did it. I dumped the Ball Buster back in the bat box, hefted Viagra with both hands, and strode to the plate. It was time for me to "push the limit."

"Hey, look who's tryin' to go deep," Eddie Nista called from the mound when he saw me with Viagra. "So, Dave, here's a sweet one for ya."

He went into his motion and delivered a beautiful pitch—slow and soft with plenty of arc. As the ball came floating in, I lunged at it with everything I had. *Ping!* The feeling was electric.

The ball jumped off the bat and sailed into the dusk. "Court, here I come" was written all over it.

Then it started to curve foul. Like Carlton Fisk in the sixth game of the '75 World Series, I hopped along the first-base line waving my arms, begging the ball to stay fair. It did, just barely. When it hit the top of the fence on the far side of the court and bounced in, I could hardly believe it. After fifteen years, I'd finally made it. I'd hit one into the court. As I broke into my home-run trot, all the old guys started giving me the needle.

"Must be a live ball tonight," Mark Tripp said at first. "Ya know, Viagra can be bad for your heart," Angelo said at second. "Think you can make it all the way around?" Paul Armington asked at short. "Ruth better watch out tonight," Tom McLaughlin said at third. "So, whatta ya gonna do for the rest of your life?" Hopie asked when I stepped on home plate.

I was wearing a grin bigger than Ryan's and was far too happy to think about the rest of my life, but as I lay in bed later that night reflecting on my new-found power, I said to Ruth, "You know, I'm going to have to come up with some new goals."

I could feel Ruth brighten up. "You could write a weekly column for a newspaper, or be a contributing editor at some magazine, or even do some corporate PR work."

"What are you talking about?" I said. "I've got to come up with some new goals for softball. You know, like hitting a grand slam, or going for the cycle, or getting the most total bases—goals that will help me push the limit. Now that I've found Viagra, I'm going deep all the time."

Whap! Ruth smacked a mosquito, rolled over, and went to sleep. But I couldn't sleep. I lay there counting softballs flying over the fence into the court at Westways. Thanks to Viagra, I felt great.

MAKE WAY
FOR JET SKIS

Obviously, my love of Maine is firmly rooted in the fifties. Our cabin, Donna's Domaine, is a throwback to Little Beaver. We still haul our drinking water in gallon jugs, now from a spring on the road to Sweden. When the three-horsepower Evinrude Ted and I bought with Dad in '55 finally conked out in '96, we didn't replace it. We went back to rowing and paddling. There are no TVs, stereos, or VCRs at the cabin. Never have been, never will be. Our only outside entertainment comes from Norway's WOXO, "92.7 on your dial, part of the Red Sox Radio Network."

My paper when I'm in Maine is *The Bridgton News,* "Serving Bridgton, Naples, Harrison, Casco, Sebago, Fryeburg, and other towns in the Lake Region of Western Maine." Lovell is one of the "other towns." The *News* comes out on Thursday, and I like to spend the morning thumbing through it, looking for church suppers, names I might recognize on the police blotter, and real estate listings on Kezar. I seldom pay much attention to the real news: accidents on Route 302, buildings hit by lightning, fires set by careless campers, or drunken brawls among canoe-ists on the Saco.

In the summer of '99, one real news item did catch my eye. The residents of Highland Lake, a popular lake in Bridgton, were trying to ban Jet Skis. The town had scheduled a nonbinding referendum for July 27. In the weeks leading up to the vote, the *News* was filled with articles, editorials, letters, and advertisements for and against the ban. Many of the letters were downright hostile, but they made good reading. I especially liked one from an old codger who claimed he was born in 1903, the year the Wright brothers invented the airplane. "If they'd banned the airplane," he said, "you wouldn't have the new and improved jets you kids fly today." He labeled the proponents of the ban "a bunch of whining 50- and 60-year old babies," and concluded by warning the people of Bridgton not to "vote away freedoms that our forefathers spilled their blood for."

My sympathies were with the people who had camps on Highland Lake. I knew firsthand how annoying Jet Skis could be. In the mid-1980s, a local guy who'd made a ton of money hanging drywall in North Conway bought a camp right opposite us on Kezar Lake. The Drywall King didn't care that the Kezar Lake Association had unanimously adopted a resolution against having any personal watercraft (PWC) on the lake. To him, the Kezar Lake Association was just a bunch of well-heeled out-of-staters, most of whom had inherited their rights to Kezar. He'd earned his, and if his kids wanted Jet Skis, they'd have them.

The little drywallers nearly drove me crazy. They'd start in the morning and go nonstop until night. *Rheeee, rheeee, rheeee,* back and forth, back and forth, back and forth. June Wing, who'd been coming to the Lower Bay since the thirties, put it best when she said, "It's like having a chainsaw in your living room."

Rodney, several guys at softball, and even the Koops, our next-door neighbors, all assured me that the Drywall King was a great guy. I didn't doubt that for a minute. Judging from the party sounds that came floating across the lake most Saturday nights, it was obvious that he liked a good time. My complaint was that he didn't tell his kids to knock it off. They got so annoying that we actually stopped going to Maine for a couple of summers. Then word drifted back that the kids had grown up and traded in their Jet Skis for kayaks. Peace had been restored to Kezar.

While I was in favor of the ban, I knew that the anti–Jet Skiers weren't going to win the referendum. The people who own most of the shoreline in the lake region of western Maine are out-of-staters. As nonresidents, they weren't eligible to vote in the election, and the locals weren't going to give up any of their rights to the lakes. Why should they? The Jet Skis weren't bothering them.

Sure enough, the headline of *The Bridgton News* for Thursday, July 29, read "Highland Lake Jet Ski ban gets sunk by 2-to-1 margin." The old codger who was so worried about his freedoms must have been very pleased. His forefathers hadn't spilled their blood in vain. Jet Skiers could continue to buzz around bothering whomever, which was too bad for the people on Highland Lake.

The following evening, Ruth and I were relaxing on the porch watching, the sun set into the White Mountains. This is our favorite time of the day, the reason we come to Maine. I'd just invited Ruth on a romantic ride in the *Ruda* when suddenly the mood was shattered by a high-pitched *rheeeeeeee*. I felt my trapezius tighten as two kids zoomed around the bend on a big red, white, and blue Jet Ski. They roared down the lake, bouncing off the sunbeams. Then back they came, looping in circles, jumping their own waves, *whack, whack, whack.* I sprang out of my wicker rocker. "Where the hell did that thing come from?"

"The next cove, I think," said Ruth.

"Impossible," I groused. "Our homeowners' association voted against Jet Skis. I'm going to have a look."

I'd never met the people who owned the house in the next cove, but according to the list published by our homeowners' association, they were from South Attleboro, Massachusetts. As I tiptoed up the driveway, I could see a humongous Ford Explorer parked next to their cabin. It had New Hampshire plates. These people obviously were renters. I ran back to report to Ruth.

"They must be renters," I said over the whine of the Jet Ski. "They're from New Hampshire."

"How do you know?"

"They have that stupid license plate, 'Live Free or Die.' If they want to live free, let 'em do it on one of their own lakes, like Winnipesaukee or Squam. Yeah, that's where they ought to go, Squam. I'm sure the people on Squam would love to have some Jet Skis buzzing around bothering their loons. After all, they were the ones who welcomed the Fondas and their film crew for *On Golden Pond*."

I picked up the receiver of our black rotary phone, the one we'd bought from AT&T in the good old days before the breakup, and dialed Joan Irish's number. Joan is president of the Kezar Lake Association (KLA). Joan doesn't tiptoe around. She's not afraid to confront anyone who's breaking the rules on Kezar.

"Joan," I said, "some kids with a Jet Ski are zooming around in front of our place. I think they're renters from New Hampshire. Don't we have a rule that says you can't rent to people with Jet Skis?"

"Where're they staying?" Joan asked.

"At that camp in the cove just up from us."

"The people who own that camp aren't members of KLA, and our homeowners' association ban is voluntary. There's nothing I can do."

Now what? Fortunately, the sun had set and darkness was creeping over the lake. *Rheeeeeee.* The Jet Ski zoomed by on what proved to be its last run. When it pulled into the cove, I could hear the kids laughing and shouting, "Man, that was awesome. I can't wait 'til tomorrow."

The Jet Ski woke me up just a little after seven. I knew I was in for a long day. *Rheeeee, rheeeee, rheeeee,* back and forth, back and forth, back and forth. First one kid, then the other, then both of them. By noon I was jumping out of my skin. When were they going to stop? Weren't they getting bored?

"Kezar's supposed to be a pristine mountain lake," I grumbled to Ruth. "These idiots are treating it like it's an amusement park. If they want to zoom back and forth all day, why don't they go to Water World in North Conway or Attitash, or wherever the hell it is."

I got my binoculars out and zeroed in on my tormentors. They were hunched over the handles with the throttle turned wide open. The looks on their faces reminded me of the kid on the bike in the children's book *Make Way for Ducklings,* the one who was going so fast he almost ran over Mrs. Mallard. These kids were having the time of their lives. They weren't going to stop for anything.

"Ruth," I said, "I can't take it any more. We've got to get outta here." I picked up *The Bridgton News* and turned to the Calendar of Upcoming Events in the lake region. "There's a church supper at the North Fryeburg Fire Station. Let's go there and then catch the early movie in Bridgton."

"What's playing?" Ruth said.

"Who cares. Anything's better than listening to that damn Jet Ski."

By the time we got back, the Jet Ski had been put away for the evening. "I sure hope those people go home tomorrow," I said. "The earlier the better. I can't take another day of that noise."

Ruth had enjoyed the firemen's supper and the movie. She'd forgotten about the noise and had turned philosophical. "They're just kids," she mused. "If you were their age, you'd be doing the same thing."

"Well, I'm not their age, and even if I were, my parents would never have let me zoom back and forth all day. They'd have made me respect other people's rights. That's the trouble with kids today. Nobody's taught them to respect other people's rights."

The next day was Sunday, the Sabbath, but thanks to the Jet Ski, it was not going to be a day of rest. The *rheeeee, rheeeee, rheeeee*ing started promptly at seven. By noon, I was at my wits' end. "If those people don't pack up and get out of here," I blustered, "I'm going to go over there and tell 'em off."

"You've got to put it out of your mind," Ruth said. "Think of it as white noise."

"White noise, my ass. It's not Muzak, it's a damn Jet Ski. I can't put it out of my mind."

"Then go for a hike. That'll calm you down."

"I'm through running, Ruth. If those idiots want noise, I'll give 'em noise." I stormed to the shed and got out my old chainsaw, a secondhand Homelite that could match any Jet Ski decibel for decibel.

"What are you doing?" Ruth asked.

"You know that big pine that was hit by lightning? I'm taking it down."

"You can't be sawing today. It's Sunday. People are trying to relax."

"Live free or die, Ruth. Live free or die."

Three hours later, the big pine was down, limbed, cut, and stacked. I took off my earmuffs and sat on the stump. The silence was deafening. What had happened to the Jet Ski? I looked over to the cove and saw the renters busily packing up the humongous Explorer. The Jet Ski was sitting on a trailer hitched to the back. I doubted that my chainsawing was driving them out, but I sure hoped so.

That evening as we sat on the porch watching the sun set, I realized that Jet Skis aren't the problem. There's always going to be some new annoyance coming around the bend: cell phones, boom boxes, car alarms, Game Boy. If I sound like one of those "whining 50- and 60-year-old babies" that the old codger described in his letter to *The Bridgton News,* it's not because I arbitrarily oppose change. What upsets me are people who don't have the concern, courtesy, or common sense to know when they're annoying their neighbors. It's a respect for nature and other people, not the fifties, that's always made my Maine so unique. Losing that respect is the change that really bothers me.

MY VIEW FROM SABBATUS

Sabbatus Mountain is not really a mountain. It's just a hill capped with granite, but its bald top provides an excellent view of the Saco River Valley. This view, and the fact that the climb is easy, makes Sabbatus one of the most popular spots in Lovell. People like to hike to the top, sit on the ledges, and contemplate the valley below.

The mountain is owned by the state but managed by the Greater Lovell Land Trust, an all-volunteer group dedicated to protecting the Kezar Lake watershed. When the land trust assumed the management of Sabbatus in 1995, the mountain was plagued with problems. Because of overuse, the upper part of the trail was seriously eroded. The lower part crossed over private property, and the landowner was sick of people tromping through his back yard and stealing water from his hose. Parking was a mess. The trailhead was off a one-lane dirt road. On busy days, cars would be scattered haphazardly along the shoulder, blocking traffic. Litter was a constant eyesore.

The land trust, at its own expense, fixed all of these problems. First, it dug drainage ditches along the upper part of the trail. Then it built a new trail to the top. This new trail forms a loop with the old trail. In addition to making the hike more interesting, the loop cuts the traffic on the old trail in half. Next the land trust rerouted the lower part of the trail over public land. Finally, it constructed a small but adequate parking lot at the base of the new trailhead. A rustic wood bulletin board at the start of the trail welcomes hikers and politely lists the dos and don'ts of Sabbatus. A trash can next to the bulletin board is emptied on a regular basis.

When a whole pack of nephews and nieces came from New Jersey for a visit, I thought that Sabbatus would be an excellent way to introduce them to the pleasures of hiking. None of these little Jerseyites had ever climbed a mountain, so I made a big deal out of our ascent. I packed a knapsack full of water, food, matches, a knife, extra socks—all the things I'd forgotten when Skipper, Lois, and I had climbed Baldface. I wanted this hike to feel like a wilderness adventure. All the way up, I kept telling the Garden Staters, "Keep your eyes open for moose and bear." They nearly jumped out of their skins when they almost stepped on a garter snake. When we reached the top and they got their first glimpse of the valley below, you would have thought they'd just conquered Everest. They were convinced they'd reached the top of the world.

"Okay," I told them, "let's walk over to the ledges. You'll be able to see the whole Saco River Valley from there. But be careful," I warned in a somber tone. "It's a long way down." They ran along the trail ahead of me, filled with excitement.

At the top of the ledges, there's an old pine tree that fell down years ago. It makes a great seat. I figured we'd sit on the pine, have some water, and eat a granola bar while I put their views into perspective by pointing out familiar landmarks.

When I caught up with the kids, they weren't sitting on the pine. They were perched on a green plastic bench. I couldn't believe my eyes. What was a plastic bench doing on the top of Sabbatus? It looked like it belonged on the boardwalk at Atlantic City.

"Where the hell did this thing come from?" I groused, ruing the loss of our wilderness experience.

The little Garden Staters looked confused. They, of course, saw nothing unusual about a tacky plastic bench. A brass plaque was attached to one of the green plastic slats. It read:

In Loving Memory
OF
Bob MacKenzie

Who was Bob MacKenzie? I'd never heard of him, but obviously somebody loved him. Putting this bench on the top of Sabbatus had been no easy task. In addition to lugging it up the mountain, whoever was honoring Bob's memory had set the bench in cement and fastened it down with nuts and bolts. That took some work.

A couple of days later, I bumped into Howard Corwin, the president of the Greater Lovell Land Trust. "Howard," I said, "who's Bob MacKenzie, and why did the land trust let somebody put that tacky plastic bench on the top of Sabbatus? It's really terrible."

"We didn't know a thing about it," Howard said. "Apparently, MacKenzie was some guy who liked the view from the top of Sabbatus. When he died, his family and friends thought they'd honor him with a bench. They never asked us if they could do it."

"Good. Then you're going to get rid of it?"

"I'm afraid not," Howard said. "They got permission from the state. We have a stewardship agreement with the state, but they never asked us what we thought about it. There's nothing we can do."

• • •

That's where I'm sitting now, on Bob's bench. Actually, it's more comfortable than the old pine tree. I can admit that because I'm here all by myself. At the beginning of August, Ruth packed up the nephews and nieces and headed south to spend a month at the Jersey Shore with her mother. Blood is thicker than water, even the crystal clear waters of Kezar. Tomorrow morning, I'm leaving to pick her up. We're going back to Virginia. My summer in Maine is over.

I never thought I could spend this much time alone, but I've gotten rather used to it. It's given me a chance to think about Maine. That's why I decided to hike up Sabbatus on my last day, to look out over the Saco River Valley and think about Maine. From Bob's bench, I can see a lot of changes in the valley, which is all the Maine I really know, yet many of the things I love have stayed the same. Much of what's stayed the same is due to the good work of the land trust.

Directly in front of me is Eastman Hill. I have a good view of the stock farm: the main house, the barn, the outbuildings, the lawns, gardens, orchards, and fieldstone walls, the flag waving from its white pole—all shimmering in the late-summer sun. A tractor's mowing one of the fields. It's a fine day to make hay, and I'm lucky to see it. If it weren't for the land trust, I'd be staring down at thirty mini-estates.

Beyond Eastman Hill, to the right, is the Lower Bay. There are some scars along the shoreline where people have cleared their lots, but from this distance, the Lower Bay looks mostly wild and untouched. That's changing. When Mom bought her lot on Ladies Delight, a summer home was a $10,000 package: $2,500 for the lot and $7,500 for the cabin. Today, a lot on the Lower Bay sells for six figures, if you can find one. Existing landowners, most of whom bought when Mom did or are related to people who did, are saying to themselves, "How can I have a $7,500 cabin sitting on a $100,000 lot?"

Many of these people are retiring and converting their cabins into year-round homes with lawns, gardens, and open vistas to the lake and mountains. Given the old real estate formula that the lot should represent a quarter to a third of the value of the house, some of these new structures are pretty fancy. Instead of being in the wilds of Maine, I'm beginning to feel that I'm part of suburbia. A home just down from us actually has a lawn service that comes in once a week. Hearing that lawnmower is a cutting reminder that Kezar isn't very wild anymore.

But the conversion of cabins into year-round homes isn't the worst of it. Given the value of lakeshore property, land that should not be developed is being developed. On Ladies Delight, right in front of our eyes, a lot that the town's code enforcement officer ruled to be undevelopable wetlands was bought by a local speculator. The speculator took down all the trees, built a boardwalk to the lake, threw up a spec house, and sold it for just under $400,000. Nobody could believe it. We all said, "How could this happen?"

The answer is simple. The speculator went around the town code enforcement officer and got a septic permit from the state Department of Environmental Protection. When the town objected, the speculator said, "Sue me." This ultimatum left the town with a simple decision: go to court and incur a lot of legal fees, or sit back and collect the taxes on a $400,000 house. Opposing a nuclear waste dump or the subdivision of a historic estate is one thing; stopping the development of one lot by a local speculator is something else. Lovell can marshal the resources for a war against outsiders, but it doesn't have the time or money to skirmish with locals.

Given the value of waterfront property, the lack of support

from the state, and the legal cost of trying to enforce codes, it's not surprising that more wetlands on Kezar are being considered for development. One plan calls for a marina to be built in an area of Sucker Brook known as the "snake pit" (we know who lives there). The marina would serve as the access point to the lake for a bundle of back lots. It's a terrible plan that would destroy the Sucker Brook marsh. That's why the plan was rejected by the town. But now the developer is threatening to sue anyone who opposes him. When I asked Howard Corwin what the land trust planned to do about it, his response was, "I try to contain my rage to one issue at a time."

Howard's current issue is milfoil, a group of water plants that can grow to depths of twenty feet. They've become so thick that swimmers can't swim, boaters can't boat, and fishermen can't fish. In time, these highly invasive aquatic plants will kill a lake. Howard calls milfoil "the AIDS of our lakes." That's a perfect analogy. Milfoil is easily spread, there is no known cure, and once a lake becomes infected, it eventually dies.

Like many threats to native natural systems, milfoil is an exotic. It was introduced to America as the green weed that pet stores put into aquariums. It went wild in the 1960s when somebody dumped a fish tank into a lake. From that moment on, milfoil has been spreading. Boats on trailers are the prime carriers, the unprotected sex. They pick up milfoil from one lake and give it to another.

Maine is one of the last states to have been infected, but Cushman Pond, right next to Kezar, is badly infested. Howard has proposed setting up checkpoints at Kezar's three public landings. He wants all boats coming onto Kezar to be washed down and their owners made aware of the threat that milfoil poses to all of Maine's lakes. Given the spread of milfoil, what

Howard's proposing seems reasonable, but he's having trouble selling the idea.

Maine's lakes are controlled by the state legislature, and without the legislature's authorization, no actions can be taken at the local level. Unfortunately, the Maine legislature has put its head in the sand when it comes to milfoil, in hopes that the problem might just go away. That's what sent Howard into a rage. "Why worry about a marina on Sucker Brook?" he fumes. "Unless we can stop the spread of milfoil, we'll lose the entire Lower Bay."

Looking farther to my right, Bob's bench provides an excellent view of the Middle Bay. It's undergoing the same changes as the Lower Bay, only on a much grander scale. A half-acre lot on the Middle Bay went on the market this year for $800,000. New money keeps flowing into Kezar, and price seems to be no object. It's become a contest to see who has the biggest boat, who has the biggest house, who has the biggest ego. Fortunately, many of the old families are granting conservation easements over their properties, and these easements are protecting large blocks of the lake shore.

Some locals worry that giving easements to the land trust will hurt the tax base, but that will never be a problem. What people will come to realize is that when a conservation easement is placed on a property, the value of that property doesn't go away. It seeps over to land that can be developed. That's why there's an $800,000 lot on the Middle Bay and a $400,000 house in a swamp on Ladies Delight. Conservation easements won't lower the tax base in Lovell. With less and less land available for development, the price of property, especially lakefront property, will go up.

If I keep turning to the right, I can almost see the Upper Bay, but not quite. Given the prices on Kezar, I know that Thursday night softball at Westways is the closest I'll ever get to the Upper Bay. For a while, I was worried about Thursday night softball. The game had started to run out of steam. Veterans like Dan McLaughlin, Stephen King, and Bob Drew had hung up their gloves, and young guys weren't showing up to fill their spots. I'm really glad women have started playing. Because they're such beautiful athletes, Mindy and Lori have injected new life into the game. I hope I can play with them for a few more years. Thanks to Viagra, maybe I can.

Sitting here on Bob's bench, it's clear that Lovell would do just fine if left to itself. It's outside forces like national organizations, state government, the federal government, exotic weeds, and exotic money that threaten to change the character of the town and the lake. How many times can one little village fight off these outside forces? The key to past victories has been locals and summer folk working together to form a united front. That's why, when people interested in conservation ask me what they can do, I tell them, "Find a good local group like the Greater Lovell Land Trust or the Kezar Lake Association or the Lovell Historical Society, write them a check, roll up your sleeves, and join the battle."

The farther out I look over the valley, the hazier things get. I imagine Horseshoe Pond will be all right. The lot restrictions the Stone sisters put in their deed have drawn some interesting people to Horseshoe. I suspect that these people have the commitment and resources necessary to keep Horseshoe from being overdeveloped.

Lovewell Pond is a different story. Even though the Reverend is gone, Jordan's Camps are still there, but the lake has become a residential community. Driving down the camp road is no longer like falling down the rabbit hole. The bumps have been leveled, the twists and turns straightened. The forest that used to be so dark and deep and quiet has been heavily logged. At the bend where we'd first see the camps, somebody has built a huge house. Across the road from the house is an ugly borrow pit where sand was excavated to build a dike around the house, I guess to buffer it against flooding. The eight little camps are still there, but there's nothing special about them. Due to all the changes on Lovewell, what used to be Wonderland is now just another overdeveloped lake.

Much the same can be said for Fryeburg. When the town lost its elms, it lost its charm. Fryeburg never made an effort to replace its trees. What it has done is install a traffic light. The light hangs over the intersection of Routes 302 and 113, winking at the monument to John Stevens, the early settler who spent the winter of 1762–63 in Fryeburg.

The White Mountain Express stopped running in 1958, the freight train soon thereafter. Today, the station's boarded up, the rails rusted, and the tracks covered with weeds and brush. Dad is gone too, but he would never beat the White Mountain Express today. The road into North Conway is one big parking lot lined with discount malls. Traffic's backed up for miles with Canadians and tourists looking for deals. If Dad took on the White Mountain Express these days, Ted and I would end up in St. Johnsbury, Vermont, for sure.

While the floor of the Saco River Valley has become clogged with cars, the surrounding peaks remain clear. From Bob's bench, I look due west at Baldface. I hiked the Circle Trail this summer. I only made four mistakes: I started late, went alone, didn't pack enough water, and forgot my AMC map. Starting late is a chronic problem, but this time it meant I was climbing in the heat of the day. When I reached the top of South Baldface, I was out of water. I thought I could borrow some from another hiker, but by the time I got to the top of North Baldface, I realized that I was going to be the last person on the summit. That meant if I tripped or fell on the way down, which would be easy to do with my new bifocals, I could be on the mountain all night.

Without my map, I got confused and once again ended up on the scenic but seldom used Bicknell Ridge Trail. If I'd fallen on that trail, nobody would've found me for a week. I made it without any problems, but I wonder when my luck on Baldface is going to run out. The real Mother Nature doesn't tolerate stupidity.

Afternoon shadows are beginning to creep over Bob's bench. It's time for me to go. The same sadness I felt whenever I left Jordan's Camps is beginning to creep over me. People are always asking me, "If you love Maine so much, why don't you move there?" They don't understand. I could never live in Maine; the winters would kill me. Between the cold and the dark, I'd be in an insulated straitjacket by Thanksgiving. What I love are the long, hot, lazy days of summer. That's *my* Maine.

Actually, I should never say never. Ruth has a plan for when I really start to lose it. "We're going to move to Maine," she says. "People there are so tolerant, it'll take them a while to realize that you've gone around the bend. When they do, I'm going to take you up to a wild river like the West Branch of the Penobscot, put you in the *Ruda,* and let you go. That way, you'll float away a happy guy."

I like that plan, especially since I don't expect it to happen anytime soon. However, one day this summer, I got up early and was going to the Center Lovell Store for the paper. It was a beautiful morning, so I decided to take a swim before I left. Since my bathing suit was downstairs, I was just wearing my shoes when I gave Ruth a nudge.

"Ruth," I said, waking her up, "I'm going to run downtown for the paper. Is there anything you want?"

Ruth rubbed her eyes, took a long look at me standing there holding the car keys, dressed in just my shoes, and said, "Get the canoe."

Give me a wave when I come floating by. That's what real Mainers do. Ayuh.